It's *All* Politics

It's *All* Politics

WINNING IN A WORLD WHERE HARD WORK
AND TALENT AREN'T ENOUGH

KATHLEEN KELLEY REARDON, PH.D.

CURRENCY   DOUBLEDAY

New York   London   Toronto   Sydney   Auckland

To Chris

PUBLISHED BY DOUBLEDAY
a division of Random House, Inc.

CURRENCY is a trademark of Random House, Inc., and DOUBLEDAY is a
registered trademark of Random House, Inc.

Book design by Michael Collica

Library of Congress Cataloging-in-Publication Data is on file with the Library of Congress.
ISBN: 0-385-50757-7

PRINTED IN THE UNITED STATES OF AMERICA

First Edition: June 2005

SPECIAL SALES
Currency Books are available at special discounts for bulk purchases for sales promotions
or premiums. Special editions, including personalized covers, excerpts of existing books,
and corporate imprints, can be created in large quantities for special needs.
For more information, write to Special Markets, Currency Books,
specialmarkets@randomhouse.com

1   2   3   4   5   6   7   8   9   10

TABLE OF CONTENTS

ACKNOWLEDGMENTS

First, my appreciation goes to Roger Scholl, editorial director at Currency Doubleday, and to my agent, Peter Ginsberg, who together made this book possible. As with my previous book on politics, *The Secret Handshake*, working with Roger and Peter has been a positive experience every inch of the way.

My appreciation goes also to my husband, Chris Noblet. He was researcher and editor on all aspects of this book and will no doubt read this acknowledgment and ask me to remove it. He is behind the scenes but front and center in deserved credit. This has been the case for many of my books, but even more for this one. When I was diagnosed with Parkinson's disease recently, I wondered whether writing was in my future. There were days of complete blur, especially while various medicines were being tried. The computer seemed a monster when once it had been a friend. Chris was there for me personally as he was professionally. He told me when something I wrote was "just not good enough," even if this was among the last things I wanted to hear. He worked tirelessly on helping me express what some days would not come, and radiated pleasure and encouragement on the days when the fog cleared and my words rushed onto the page. This book is dedicated to Chris, as is my abiding love.

Sarah Rainone at Currency Doubleday edited this book with impressive commitment. She is a true reader's advocate in her quest for clarity, even while endeavoring to preserve the author's style and voice. She is a rising star and I was glad to benefit en route. I am also grateful to Sean Mills, Nora Reichard, Lawrence Krauser, Michael Collica, Luisa Francavilla, Umi Kenyon, and Laine Kavanaugh at Doubleday, and to Debby Manette for her skilled copyediting.

My appreciation goes to the hundreds of people who've told me their political stories. Some are named in this book, others given fictional names at their request.

I want to thank my children, Shannon, Ryan, and Devin. Devin makes me laugh when I least expect it. I treasure those laughs and the times when the dishes were miraculously done or a room was suddenly clean. Ryan is considerate and inquisitive. We often just sit and talk at length about a subject that has captured his interest. As he says, we share a "very special bond." Shannon's enthusiasm for life and her spontaneous hugs brighten my days. Among her many interests, she wants to become a writer someday. This book is written with the fond hope that it will help them manage the politics in their own lives. My thanks also to all the members of my family, both immediate and extended, who continue to encourage me to write.

My friends always participate in what I write whether they share their experiences or encourage me in other ways. Thanks also to my colleagues at the University of Southern California, the Irish Management Institute, and University College, Cork, who have shared their knowledge of politics. While on leave from USC in Schull, Ireland, I was also blessed with the friendship of artists in the community, including Ann Stalberger, whose watercolors are superb, and who has been my encouragement and my mentor. To Peter Samuelson, Claudia Kennedy, and Debbie Sams of Washington, D.C.–based First Star devoted to the protection and advancement of children's rights, I hope this will be a banner year when political walls of injustice and indifference crumble and children who live in harm's way will be better served.

CHAPTER ONE

IT'S ALL POLITICS

L IKE BUSINESS IN general, politics is not a spectator sport. You cannot afford to be apolitical at work if you have any aspirations for advancement. The only way to avoid politics is to avoid people — by finding an out-of-the-way corner where you can do your job. Of course, it's the same job you'll likely be doing for the rest of your career if you remain politically impaired.

In any job, when you reach a certain level of technical competence, politics is what makes all the difference with regard to success. At that point, it is indeed all politics. Everyday brilliant people take a backseat to politically adept colleagues by failing to win crucial support for their ideas.

Sometimes politics involves going around or bending rules, but more typically it's about positioning your ideas in a favorable light and knowing what to say, and how, when, and to whom to say it. Refusing to participate in what you may consider "the incivility of politics" is exactly what will keep you a political underdog, watching helplessly as your career aspirations evaporate.

Ask yourself these questions to see if you're up to snuff on politics 101.

- Can you effectively influence and manage people's perceptions of you and your ideas?
- Are you able to convert enemies to allies?

- Can you manage outcomes long before they're in sight?
- Do your ideas get a fair hearing?
- Do you know when and how to present them?
- Are you in the loop?

If you've answered no to even one of these questions, you can learn a great deal from this book. Such political skills determine career success, but they are only the beginning. Politics is a highly complex skill set. Albert Einstein was once asked: "Dr. Einstein, why is it that when the mind of man has stretched so far as to discover the structure of the atom we have been unable to devise the political means to keep the atom from destroying us?" The great scientist replied: "That is simple, my friend. It is because politics is more difficult than physics."[1]

Politics is more difficult than physics because most of us have not devoted adequate time to the study of it. Most business schools disregard politics completely, even though the success of their students will depend to a large extent on their political skill level. This is the case for the elite scientist as well as the machinist working on a shop floor. Business schools generally ignore an entire type of human intelligence in favor of more technical subjects, and many otherwise talented people suffer as a result. They bumble their way through the workplace, saying whatever is on their minds or failing to say that which they should because they never learned the difference.

Security at work comes from being able to manage how people treat you and your ideas. This is true no matter where you are on the hierarchy. I worked with a CEO who'd been in place for less than a year when he realized that certain board members were out to get him. When I met him, he was moderately political, no match for the masters on his board. They were becoming so effective in their attempts to unseat him that even his most ardent supporters were beginning to waver. This CEO invited me to work with him on his communication. He made no mention of altering his political approach. But soon it became evident that this man was about to walk the plank if he didn't learn how to manage belowdecks as well as at the helm. After meeting with his direct reports, I learned from them, as well as from him, about each board member's agendas and political styles. The CEO and I then looked at each board member's alliances and discussed at length what had been said at prior meetings, especially those statements that seemed to be undermining his position.

If I had thought that this CEO was a threat to the company, I wouldn't have agreed to help him see past his own nonpolitical predilections. But his employees truly admired him and what he'd already achieved. They considered the board's behavior to be the result of sour grapes among a couple of members who'd wanted to hire a different CEO. But some employees were beginning to lose respect for this CEO because he couldn't seem to stifle or appease his adversaries. Workdays were becoming fractious, with less work getting done as senior people spent more time worrying about their jobs than doing them.

After I convinced the CEO that he needed to learn how to manage his board politically, I began the process of teaching him how to present himself and his ideas. We discussed which board members he should call before each meeting and which ones would provide him with the insights we needed to formulate a strategy. Interestingly, it became clear that the most important issue was the need some members felt to have their opinions valued by the new CEO. They also wanted reassurance that they would retain the power they perceived themselves to be losing. Another issue for them was a feeling that the CEO lacked conviction and self-confidence. Over a period of several weeks I worked with the CEO to alter these damaging perceptions. I sat in his office while he spoke with the leaders of the insurgency, assuring them not only that he'd heard their suggestions but also, in two instances, planned to put them in charge of implementation. We worked on his style, on his sense of conviction, on the words he'd use at the next board meeting, on positioning ideas and past events in a positive way, and on how he'd address, call on, and respond to all members of the board. We identified areas of agreement that could be emphasized. We even practiced in the boardroom with certain trusted senior managers playing the roles of his detractors. Yes, it was a lot of work, but so is learning physics—and, remember, according to Einstein, physics is easier. The reluctant politician proved to be a fast learner. The insurgency ended and a good man's career was saved.

Whether at the very top of organizations or farther down the ladder, the politically astute stay in touch with what is going on around them and communicate with others in ways that align their goals with those in power or soon to be in power. They make it their business to know a great deal about the systems in which they work, the common views that define those systems as well as loopholes in those common views, and the kind of behavior considered contro-versial. They know how to talk so that others are compelled to lis-ten. Well in advance of any serious conflict, they develop an arsenal of options and a corral of connections that can help make those op-tions possible.

You can't know politics simply by discussing it theoretically. I learned what I know by observing, trying new approaches, falling on my face, and getting up to try again. One of my very early polit-ical lessons came from a colleague who, after seeing me struggle with a manipulator, took me aside and said, "He doesn't need to be confronted; he needs to be managed. He's predictable and quite needy, really," she continued, an interpretation that seemed foreign to me at the time, not to mention surprising, considering it was re-garding someone so much my senior. "He has you where he wants you: desperate to please, easily hurt by his rebuffs because you sim-ply haven't stopped to think. Give him some of what he wants—be less predictable yourself. Try a little unexpected kindness and guide him to your side. He's not your friend, but you're making him an enemy. And that's where you're losing the game."

As an alumna of the University of Connecticut, I watch as many UConn basketball games as possible. In 2004 the men and women both won NCAA championships. It was the first time in history that men's and women's teams from the same school won this honor.

Sports Illustrated describes star player Diana Taurasi this way: "What everybody says, one way or another, is that Taurasi sees. She sees things on the court that God hasn't arranged for other people to pick out."[2] This is what intuition is about—seeing more and farther ahead than others. Truly effective politicians possess an uncanny sense of their surroundings. Small nonverbal moves, changes in the direction of talk, and momentary emotional expressions do not escape them. Information that seems peripheral to most people is often pivotal for the intuitive, whether on a basketball court or in a critical business meeting. The real stars in any endeavor are those who see—truly see—and then use that information to determine their course of action. Novices operate in the dark, some desperately attempting to pick up a strategy here or there, but until they see what is really going on around them, no amount of strategy accumulation will advance them.

One media executive told me she developed a sense of what's ahead over time. "I now know if there's a big hole in the ground up ahead. I don't need to go put my foot in it anymore." This book will teach you how to develop an early warning system for detecting when something in the environment just isn't right—when there's a hole up ahead. You'll learn that skilled politicians listen to their gut while so many others push valuable impressions aside.

I'll also explore how to detect deception—a look at primates can teach us a great deal about being aware of dangers that lurk nearby. As primatologist Franz de Waal has discovered, chimpanzees don't make uncalculated moves. They are always keeping track of each other, always thinking about the next social step.[3] Chimps form coalitions and work together to assess their surroundings and deal with potential enemies. We humans tend to keep track mostly of ourselves, especially in western cultures, and pride ourselves on individual, rather than group, accomplishment. Because of this, we lower our chances of truly seeing what is going on around us. Fortunately, with time and practice, you'll be less inclined to readily dismiss a nagging sense that something isn't quite right. You'll learn how to listen to your gut and make sense of the input. This is a crucial step in becoming politically skilled and advancing your career. Like Diana Tarausi's sense of the court, we all need to develop a keen sense of our work surroundings in order to take some impressive shots when others are still looking for the ball.

Once you have developed intuition, you also need to have the insight to respond creatively to a variety of situations. The worst thing you can be at work is predictable. When you are, people can easily manage and maneuver around you. Skilled politicians have an extensive repertoire of responses so they're prepared for anything. They know that there is more than one way to handle any situation; for every locked entrance, there is a back door, windows—even a chimney. I'll discuss how to determine which concerns should be on your front burner and a variety of responses to those concerns. You'll learn to be flexible and creative in your responses in order to avoid falling into a predictable routine. I'll show you how to break out of these ruts to find fresh ways of dealing with problems at work.

You also will learn how to better prepare yourself for political situations at work before they happen. People who speak first take a big risk in politically volatile situations, unless they're well prepared. The magic in being politically savvy lies in advance work, not in fancy strategies. You have to learn to be on the lookout for situations that could be harmful to your career. Skilled politicians have multiple antennae taking in information that others overlook or discard. They go from room to room dusting for fingerprints, asking questions when others don't. You have to know what makes the people with whom you're dealing tick.

You also will master the skill of thinking on your feet. People constantly tell me they think of what they *should* have said at some point of the workday only when they're driving home from work; but, of course, it's already too late. On their feet, most people are a disaster. The good news is that this condition can be changed. You *can* learn to dance, even late in life. When you learn how to think strategically, you can jump into the fray and walk away with everything you wanted—or pretty darn close.

Politics is nothing without acquiring the power of persuasion. Persuasion is not something you do, it's something you work at doing. Emeka Okafor, star of the UConn men's national championship team, didn't start playing basketball until he was in the sixth grade. A few years later, he was on the highest-ranked college team in the United States. What happened between sixth grade and his first year at UConn can be summed up in one word: work. He focused on learning from the best—his coach Jim Calhoun, his teammates, and his adversaries—just as his father had focused on earning several advanced college degrees. You can't pick up a few tricks and expect to reach the corner office one day—or to stay there once you arrive. And if you can't influence others, then the road ahead is a short one.

Politics is often associated with power as if they're one and the same. If I had to choose between persuasion and power as the heart of politics, I'd choose persuasion. Yet power is a critical component of career politics. People pay attention to those they *perceive* to be powerful. I say "perceive" because power is largely in the eye of the beholder. It's created through relationships rather than status alone. Even people of low status can have and accrue power. They just need to understand how to attain it and use it effectively.

Just as you'll learn ways to develop power in an organization, you'll also come to recognize moments when you'll need to be courageous. Sticking your neck out is never an easy thing in life. After all, the tall tree catches the wind. But you'll see how some impressive people turned bad situations to good by having the guts and the skill to step forward in crisis situations. We'll look at what it takes to be politically courageous—both the prerequisites and the means—and we'll examine how people who commit career suicide miss the mark.

Politics is inevitable. It is part of life. But that doesn't have to be a bad thing. Many companies have made efforts to manage politics in productive ways. They haven't tried to stamp out political activity so much as they've rewarded positive politics. They've helped individuals find their own political compasses, and the results are impressive not only in terms of those organizations' cultures, but in terms of the bottom line as well. Once the idea that there is such a thing as positive politics sinks in, organizations and individuals can encourage it and discourage harmful political machinations.

You'll know a lot more about the supposed "mystery" that is politics when you finish this book. Keep in mind that people benefit from perpetuating the image of politics as something you either know or you don't. Ignore them.

Political acumen is largely learned from observation. And then it's a matter of practice, practice, and more practice. When a journalist suggested that golfing great Gary Player was very lucky, he replied: "It's funny, but the more I practice the luckier I get." The same is true of politics.

CHAPTER TWO

POLITICAL INTUITION

IS THERE SOMETHING inherently special about politically skilled people? Do they possess, by nature, an uncanny ability to sense what others fail to see? Do they instinctively know when to take a new approach to a complex problem? And if so, does that mean that no matter how much the rest of us study and practice politics, we'll never achieve real political savvy?

Intuition, political or otherwise, is indeed something special. It's a skill possessed by a minority of people who approach communication attentively. They are high-level thinkers who take little for granted and avoid the common tendency to slip into destructive patterns. Most important, these people are far less predictable than the rest of us.

Consider, for example, what you do when someone says "Hi, how are you?" when he walks by. In all likelihood your reply is brief; perhaps you say "Fine. How are you?" By the time you've finished that brief utterance, the distance between you and the other person may be too great for him to reply. Besides, chances are you didn't really want to know the answer, and he cared little about your response. If he had, he would have stopped to receive your answer. The two of you were merely enacting a greeting ritual—an exchange of courtesies. Much of our daily interaction with people is scripted in such ways. Many of the things we say and do in our daily routines have become so habitual that little thought goes into them. Rather than being consciously initiated, they usually are cued by something someone else says or does. After years of learning ways to respond to typical situations, we cease to consider whether an alternative approach might be more productive. Once we really get to know people, this type of automatic response becomes dysfunctional—we become trapped in these played-out scripts. It makes me yawn just to think about such dull conversations. These dysfunctional communication patterns (DCPs) prevent us from seeing situations with a fresh eye. The following conversation is an example of a DCP.

> **Susan:** I felt dismissed in that meeting, John.
>
> **John:** Now, Susan, don't get emotional.
>
> **Susan:** I believe you interrupted me three times.
>
> **John:** No! I wouldn't do that. But if you're going to take forever to formulate a thought, people aren't going to wait.
>
> **Susan:** I didn't take that long.
>
> **John:** Susan, it's not that big a deal. You're overreacting. And you look tired.
>
> **Susan:** I'm fine.
>
> **John:** Okay, okay—why don't we talk about this some other time when you're up to it?

It's easy to imagine Susan having these kinds of conversations with people on a regular basis—many of us come to rely on such scripts without realizing our folly. Let's look at Susan's mistakes and how she could have avoided them. First, she starts the conversation with a description of how she feels. This gives John the opening to discuss her feelings rather than the issue of interruptions. When Susan does mention her concern about John's interruptions, she does so meekly. Does she "believe" he interrupted her, or does she know he did? There's a difference. Had she said, "John, you interrupted me three times," she would have made her case and limited John's choices of how to respond. Instead, she has given him the option to deny her vague allegation and define the situation in a more assertive way. Her reply, once again, is not sufficient to achieve her goal of bringing about a change in his actions. She refers to what she "thinks" happened instead of what she knows happened. Her meek approach allows John to blame her emotional state and, once again, dodge the main issue. By then her assertion, "I'm fine," is too late to cause him to revise his patronizing approach.

Throughout this conversation, there are what I call "choice points"—moments when either Susan or John could alter its course. By abdicating her responsibility to protect her image, Susan helps create the DCP. She allows John to put her down, never once addressing the issue she's raised, and allows him to focus instead on her emotions. Susan could have altered this patronizing DCP at several points if she had previously prepared a repertoire of direct comments. She might have started the conversation by saying "John, I didn't appreciate your interruptions today," or "Listen, John, please don't interrupt me at a meeting again." If these comments are beyond her level of assertiveness, she might have said, "John, I'm extending you the courtesy of coming here to discuss today's meeting. But be assured that if you continue to interrupt me, I'm going to respond in kind." That would have gotten his attention. An even less direct comment might be "John, we need to talk."

Even if Susan does fail to start her conversation with John by directly focusing on the issue, she still can alter its course. After John criticized the time it takes her to formulate thoughts, she might have said, "My timing isn't the issue here, John. The issue is your interruptions," or "John, please stop dodging the issue." Even toward the end of the conversation, when John mentions her fatigue, she could bring about a better ending by saying "You're way off the subject, John. Next time we're in a meeting, please don't cut me off," or "We're not discussing my emotional state. We're talking about why you interrupted me." If John were to continue his patronizing DCP by saying they should meet again when she's more rested, Susan could say, "We need to fix this now, John, before the next meeting," or "Let's not change the subject. Please do not interrupt me again."

People like Susan who rely heavily on scripts make themselves predictable. By helping others to know what to expect of them, they're giving up the upper hand in managing their interactions and relationships. You see, people who pay attention to such patterns in communication quickly realize when someone is dependent on scripts. This knowledge allows them to predict how people who stick to scripts are likely to react.

Developing intuition, political or otherwise, requires an ability to observe patterns and an openness to many types of information, including emotional cues. Unfortunately, from an early age, most of us are taught to be suspicious of information that is not practical. Since our gut feelings seem to originate from the emotional side of ourselves, we often treat them as fuzzy, ungrounded, and untrustworthy. At the same time, we admire intuitive people for being able to "read" such information.

Intuitive people don't possess magical abilities or extrasensory perception; they've simply learned to perform "gut checks." When they sense something awry, they do not dismiss their hunches—they stop and ask if something is amiss. Shakti Gawain, author of *Developing Intuition*, believes that many of us have programmed our intellects to doubt our intuitions. "When an intuitive feeling arises, our rational minds immediately say, 'I don't think that will work,' or 'What a foolish idea,' and the intuition is disregarded."[1] This kind of thinking is due to our society's emphasis on pure intellect. The trouble with pure intellect is that it often allows us to take in only a portion of relevant information. Intuitive people, on the other hand, tend to multitrack. They take in information from a variety of sources (e.g., words, gestures, tone of voice, environment) and process it in more advanced ways than other people. Their complex observations generate more choices and open more doors for effective communication than those trapped by logic or objectivity.

POLITICAL ADVANTAGE #1

Political intuition is not uncanny clairvoyance but rather uncanny attentiveness to what others say and how they act.

If you're politically intuitive, you'll sense when a policy change is afoot because of your attentiveness to clues that others miss. You'll know before others do when people are lying, wiggling out of a commitment, setting you up for a fall, covering their backs, or making themselves look good at your expense. The more intuitive you are, the earlier you'll recognize such behaviors. Once you develop what might be called a *political early warning system*, it will be hard to get much by you. Your political antennae will be on high alert and ready to take in important information.

People who are politically naive have few, if any, antennae. They walk around unconsciously letting life happen to them. They're pushed and pulled through life because they're so often blindsided by events that politically astute people anticipate. They simply don't see political disaster coming.

At one time I was such a person, until a good friend was kind enough to point this out. One day after I'd stumbled into a political minefield at work, where I was the target of a person determined to make himself look good at my expense, my friend said, "Kathleen, you have an amazing capacity to see way in advance that the shit is about to hit the fan." At this point I was quite complimented, but alas, my well-meaning friend continued. "The trouble is you doubt yourself. You wonder if perhaps you might be wrong, if you're being too critical of the people involved. You then accord them every consideration and stick around to see if they were worthy and — splat — you're a target." Despite my feeble protestations, I knew my friend was right. "As if that weren't enough," he continued, "you arise from the slaughter and deny, despite your keen awareness to the contrary, that such a horror could ever happen again. You stand on a chair to get a better look, and lo and behold, it does."

I've never forgotten that criticism. Although it was painful to hear, it had a significant, positive effect on my future. I taught myself to be more trusting of my hunches, especially the educated ones. I stopped stepping into the line of fire in spite of early warning danger signals. I learned to put my talent to use. It's important that you do the same. After a few years in a political work environment, you should be able to recognize danger is lurking.

The politically intuitive have many antennae. Information comes to them in many forms and from many sources. They are connoisseurs of politics because their information receiving capacity is advanced. The good news is that political skills can be learned.

TAKING LITTLE AT FACE VALUE

I've already discussed the importance of being wary of assumptions. You can't develop political intuition without adopting an inquisitive approach to your dealings with people. You can't believe, as so many people do, the last thing you heard just because it was the most recent. Nor can you afford to rely on stereotypes and untested assumptions about people and what they say.

Politically intuitive people ask lots of questions. "Why do you think that? Have you considered other options? Is there more here than meets the eye? Are there alternative ways to look at this?" They don't react before observing and thinking about multiple ways that a situation might be interpreted. They take an inordinate interest in people, not simply because they're more considerate or curious than the rest of us, but because they've trained themselves to learn before judging, to consider before acting. They aren't slow, even though their inquisitiveness occasionally may cause them to appear so. In fact, they move quite dexterously through this observation/ inquiry process.

How did they get this way? Or more to the point, how can *you* get this way if you're not already there? I tell the students in my MBA courses that they need to develop a *red-flag alert* that warns them when they're doing more telling than asking and/or more assuming than inquiring. When you become aware that you're making snap judgments or failing to ask enough questions, STOP! Immediately substitute questions for assumptions when speaking with people. Ask about them. Find out what *they* think, as opposed to what you assume they think. The distinction is critical. Start the hard way. Try this with someone whom you know well, whose intentions you usually judge quite quickly. This next time you talk with her, try to see her in a new way. Take an interest in her perspective, not what you assume it to be. Likely you'll discover that you didn't know her at all, that there is much more to what she says than meets the eye, and that you've been duped by your own hasty assumptions!

The next step is to make this new inquisitive approach a part of your style. You don't have to ask people what they really mean when they said "Hello." There isn't always a hidden meaning. But the next time you're having a conversation and something doesn't ring true, if the outcome is likely to have a significant impact on your life or career, be much more inquisitive. Be sure not to make your questions sound like a quiz. And choose ones likely to provide you with valuable information.

Speed in decision making is rarely as important as having enough information. Learning how to get additional and crucial information without getting sidetracked is critical in the development of political intuition. I emphasize this point every semester and in every training session, yet most people enter into negotiation and politics role-plays thinking of what they're going to *tell* the other person rather than what they're going to *ask*. It's useful to know your best arguments, but it's not as important as learning how the other side thinks. Without questions, your so-called best arguments will be easily shot down.

The CEO I coached to better relations with his board had the unfortunate habit of trying to demonstrate his competence and leadership ability by running roughshod over those who disagreed with him in public. For him, questions constituted weakness. And so he would tell rather than ask, which caused his enemies to increase their disdain for him. He worked on curbing this dysfunctional reaction by thinking about what he wanted to say moments before telling anyone anything and before he felt the desire to reply in a contentious manner. These infinitesimal moments of thought made all the difference. When a board member angrily said to this

CEO, "That won't work. We tried it," the CEO paused before replying "What would you have done differently now that you know that it didn't work?" This type of question renders the critic an expert, keeps the topic under discussion, and might lead to a constructive evaluation of how to make a success of a former failed attempt. The CEO might have asked, "What was learned from that failure?" or "Was any aspect of that experience successful?" Both of these questions are valiant attempts to salvage some aspect of the proposed plan.

At the very least, questions buy time. They interrupt the tendency many of us share of wanting to appear to be an expert and allow us to rescue a topic from premature demise. They have the added advantage of providing valuable information or clarity. In all these ways questions are a politician's secret weapon, underused by novices, used often and effectively by experts.

LEARNING HOW THINGS ARE DONE AROUND HERE

One of the first things a politically intuitive person does on encountering a situation is observe whether what is happening is normally expected. Knowing how "things are done around here" is critical to career survival. Intuition involves sensing when something isn't quite right. For example, in some organizations, "reorganizing" is actually a euphemism for impending layoffs. When a McKinsey rep comes to your door, it isn't to learn more about you and discover your hidden talents. He or she may not be carrying an ax, but you probably are on the list of potential cuts. Anyone who's been around for a while knows a McKinsey visit is rarely a good sign. But if you are young and inexperienced, likely you won't know what to do in such a situation.

Signs of impending peril are not always so obvious, however, even to the experienced. But new people run a greater risk of misdiagnosing a politically precarious situation. Those who've been around for a while might know, for example, that a discussion at a departmental meeting has likely been preceded by a backroom discussion involving a few key people. In such cases, entering into the discussion thinking your comments actually might make a difference is politically naive. If you want to make a difference, you must make your contribution earlier.

The processes by which people are promoted, demoted, edged out, and selected for prize project teams and plum assignments is usually repetitive. Becoming more intuitive involves increasing your mastery of *pattern recognition*. This means learning to interpret events in an "if-then" fashion. In other words, in the past, when X occurred, was it usually followed by Y or Z? Make it your mission to find out what your coworkers did before getting a raise or getting fired. If one or two people promoted were seen at lunch with a particular senior executive weeks before, take note of that. I once advised a colleague to invite such a person to lunch not long before a promotion decision was to be made about him. He decided that his record spoke for itself, and he wanted no part of a move he saw as opportunistic. My view was that a lunch couldn't hurt, and, in fact, that it might help. Besides, he didn't need to sell his soul—it was just a lunch. I knew from experience that his boss liked having junior people ask him for advice. He gave it willingly, but unless you consulted him, he would not search you out, nor would he stick his neck out to get you promoted. I knew that his opinion carried a good deal of weight. My colleague chose to dine elsewhere and was not promoted. Despite his stellar record, his failure to recognize a pattern cost him the support that almost certainly would have put him over the top. And to think, a mere hour out of one day might have made all the difference.

Whenever a decision important to your career is about to be made, it helps considerably to ask those who've been around for a while how your chances might be enhanced. Here are some questions you can ask.

- Are there people I can speak to who will help me get promoted?

- When and how should the idea of my being promoted be advanced?
- Whose toes should I avoid stepping on?

This kind of knowledge comes only from the wisdom of experience. It's a source of intuition that can be obtained only through direct observation over time or borrowed from those who've seen it all before.

READING BETWEEN THE LINES

I was hired as a coach to advise some up-and-coming junior executives headed for bright futures. "What they really need," I was told, "is the ability to read between the lines." One of these young people had the particular misfortune of being totally blind to any but the most obvious messages. He couldn't take a hint, follow a hunch, read innuendo, or see past a compliment to a criticism. For this reason, his superiors worried, and rightly so, that his future was compromised.

The first step in learning to read between the lines is to recognize that communication operates on two levels of meaning: content and relational. Content meaning refers to what is actually said. Relational meaning refers to what is said, or more often implied, regarding the relationship between the persons involved. It is difficult to read meaning into a conversation because people engage in myriad forms of deception on both levels. From a very early age we are discouraged from being completely honest in our communication. Although this indirectness is more prevalent in some cultures than in others, it exists everywhere. The idea of "the truth and nothing but the truth" is generally reserved for courtrooms, and even there it is difficult to achieve. As social beings—that is, as people who rely on the goodwill of others for affection, inclusion, and control—we cannot afford to say whatever is on our minds. As a result, many of us develop indirect ways of saying what we mean or asking for or demanding what we want. We cloak demands in the guise of advice, criticism in the robe of constructive guidance.

One very important skill is the ability to recognize when a "disconnect" exists between what is said and what is meant. "You've done quite a job here" could be taken as a compliment. At face value that is what it appears to be. But what if this comment was said with a sneer or rolled eyes? The meaning would be quite different. Yet if challenged, the eye-roller could say, "Clearly I was complimenting her." Clearly indeed! Very few things are clear in communication. Understanding is always a matter of interpretation, especially when politics enters the mix. "You certainly came on strong in that meeting" could be a compliment, but just as easily a put-down. "No one should mess with you" might be seen as an expression of admiration or as a subtle hint to change your style. Accuracy in determining other people's true meanings depends on the ability to read beyond the more obvious content.

If a coworker tells you "You certainly deserve respect for your determined stance," it may mean that she holds you in high esteem. If the emphasis is on the word "respect," however, and nonverbal cues suggest some disconnect, she might be hinting that you deserve respect for your effort, but little else. "Are you feeling okay today?" may be a sincere inquiry about health. But if it's said publicly or after you've criticized a coworker's proposal, that same comment might have been intended to cause you discomfort or embarrassment. These simple examples demonstrate how complex communication is and how easily an innocent, sincere-sounding comment can be used in a deceitful way.

Perhaps by now you're thinking that you could easily become paranoid spending your entire day thinking of alternative meanings and ulterior motives. But if you operate in a highly or pathologically political environment, a small amount of paranoia can be protective. Even in minimally political arenas, communication often is conducted in this manner. This is why sharpening your intuitive skills is so important. If you're just starting out at your job, find some mentors who know how things are said and done. After meetings, find time to meet with them. Listen to what they have to say about what actually went on. Did you interpret comments in ways similar to theirs? Did you miss a lot of what was implied? Choose your mentors wisely, and don't advertise that you are studying the communication habits of your colleagues. They might cease to talk in your presence.

After a while you'll start to develop red flags that alert you to disconnects. You'll begin to notice (if you don't already) when something is being implied but not said. You'll notice too when a comment seems too out of place to be taken at face value. Most important—and this is where even the sensitive observers can go wrong if they fail to trust themselves—you'll learn to heed your internal warning signals. Many good observers dismiss their observations, telling themselves that they're being too sensitive. They deny their own intuition, responding only to the surface meaning of the comments. As a habit, this is a waste of talent and a likely route to a disappointing career.

When you notice a disconnect, pause. Make sure you understand what was meant. This may require that you ask a question. "I'm not sure that I completely understand what you're saying" is one way to figure out an implied meaning. "Should I take what you said to mean that I need to change my ways?" is another. "I appreciate the advice" can be useful when something said seemed to be a message of criticism. If the other person replies with "What advice? I was merely complimenting you," you might say, "And I appreciate that," or "I know, but I benefited from what you said in ways you didn't intend." You have to be careful here, because you too communicate on two levels. The way *you* say things is also more important than what you're saying. Nonverbal gestures can turn innocent comments into fighting words. If there's a hint of sarcasm in your tone, the other person likely will notice it.

The following simple conversation demonstrates how the disconnect between what is said and what is meant can be addressed with constructive questions. Read it, and practice on your own with someone you trust.

Sharon: I think that meeting went well.

Marie: *(nods with no eye contact)*

Sharon: We covered all that we needed to cover and then some.

Marie: That's true.

Sharon: You're rather noncommittal. Is something wrong?

Marie: Not really.

Sharon: Something is bothering you. Tell me.

Marie: We might have covered a lot, but we resolved very little.

Sharon: I thought we reached closure on several issues.

Marie: We did, but they were minor ones. They were shallow victories, not real ones.

Sharon: Why did you wait until now to bring this up?

Marie: There never seemed to be a good moment. Besides, we can still propose an additional meeting to resolve the major issues. I sensed from everyone's lack of elation when we finished today that they'd be receptive to this.

Sharon: Okay. Let's do it.

This simple conversation could have gone quite differently had Sharon not noticed Marie's lack of enthusiasm and asked Marie to explain what was wrong. So much information is lost when people assume they know how others are thinking instead of asking them. But quick surface readings of someone's words won't tell you their meaning, especially in situations where emotions are involved.

Even in e-mails, what is written is not always what is meant. Some disconnects may result from poor or rushed communication; others are due to moods. Over e-mail it can be difficult to sort out the difference between a bad day and an intentionally offensive message. Sorting it out is critical, however, if you want to reply in a politically astute manner. Once again, when in doubt, ask a question. "I noticed some tension in your last e-mail. Is there something wrong?" might be one approach. If you have some idea of what might be wrong, another approach is "My apologies for the abrupt tone in responding last time. I was distracted by six phone calls in a row." See how the person responds. Don't react with an apology if it's unnecessary. Save it for times when you should apologize. No doubt there will be enough of them. "How are things with you?" can move a conversation away from work issues and allow you to determine if something is indeed bothering the person and whether it has to do with you. If you detect a problem, whether it's relevant to your actions or not, it may be time to pick up the phone or to walk over to the person's office. E-mail is woefully limited when it comes to dealing with emotional or complex issues, but taking the time to speak to a colleague shows your concern. Given how quickly so many e-mails are dashed off, there is considerable room for error in interpretation, and it's better to err on the side of caution.

Next are two examples of how a dashed-off e-mail can threaten relationships:

Jim: I've been working on our project overtime each night. I'm sitting here in the office at 9 P.M. as I've done so many nights, and no one is here but me. When you arrive tomorrow, we need to find some kind of equitable solution to the work imbalance. I can't carry all the weight here. You've done some good things, but it simply isn't enough to get the report done on time and at the level of quality expected. Get back to me today. We need to resolve this right away.

Maxine

This e-mail is an example of failed politics. First, why did Maxine use e-mail to express her opinion on a delicate topic like this? She wrote the e-mail at 9 P.M., when she was obviously tired and feeling put upon. She doesn't appear to have asked any questions regarding Jim's view of things. She formulated assumptions and dumped them untested into a contentious e-mail. There is also the issue of wording. Maxine should never have sent this e-mail, but instead should have treated it as catharsis—a way of getting her opinion off her chest and onto paper, where she could then edit and refine it. Her next step should have been to delete it and start over. Here is how she might have achieved her purpose by e-mail.

> Jim: Let's meet tomorrow morning. I've been working on the project the last several nights and want to share with you what I have and determine together how to proceed. Does 9 A.M. work for you?
>
> Maxine

That's all Maxine should have put in her e-mail. She should save her feelings about being overworked for the face-to-face meeting and not discuss them there unless absolutely necessary. If she begins the meeting with an explanation of the work she's done, Jim may decide to talk about his contributions so far. In the light of day, she may no longer feel the way she'd felt the night before. Perhaps Jim has done quite a bit already and has not shared that with Maxine. He may think that he contributed early on in the project and that now it is her turn. She needs to assess these factors before expressing emotions, implying unfairness or laziness. If she still feels that Jim is not pulling his weight, she should tell him so in face-to-face conversation.

Let's look at a more complex situation in which misunderstandings have occurred, where the two people work in different offices and one of them prefers to communicate by e-mail. In this example, their departments are working on the same project. The advertising segment for a new product launch was just completed, and the costs were submitted to the project team leader, a marketing analyst named Tom. He's not pleased. Tom writes a memo to Erica, an advertising associate, and copies it to the senior VP of operations.

> Erica: The budget for advertising just came across my desk. I don't know what you people are up to over there, but it isn't worth the cost you specified. It's way over what we allocated. Who signed off on this? This isn't the first time I've had this

happen and we've had to pull in our belts to make up for advertising overspending. Not this time. I won't pay this. You'll have to swallow $30,000. Next time stay within the budget or don't bother doing the work. We can outsource for less.

Tom
Cc: Rob Milton

If you were Erica, what would you do? I hope you wouldn't rush to reply. The person you report to should be brought into the loop, as he or she is likely to hear about this anyway and may want to offer some input. Given that Tom has copied the memo to Rob Milton, a senior vice president, you need to consider how he'll respond. Does Rob know Tom as someone who shoots from the hip, so to speak, or does he respect him? Does advertising have a track record of going over budget, and, if so, how often and by how much? Is Tom someone who gets steamed and later cools down and apologizes, or is this atypical for him? If the former is true, then you could merely send a brief memo back to him saying:

Tom: I'll look into the budget issue and get back to you ASAP.

Erica

Your manager may want to go see the senior VP or perhaps bring you along. Instead of belittling Tom, you both should start the meeting with the facts and stick to them. Why did you go over the budget? Was there permission to do so? If not, why not? Has marketing picked up the slack in the past because of advertising overrides? Is there something your department has done that evens the score? If you're fortunate, Rob may advise you with regard to responding to Tom. He may suggest a meeting rather than dueling e-mails. But if an e-mail is needed, it should look something like this:

Tom: We've looked over the budget with Rob. There were some additional expenses but no one expects marketing to

have to shoulder those. If that were the case, you'd be
absolutely right to object. Our departments have worked
together exceptionally well in the past and we have every
intention of ensuring that we continue to do so. Let's meet soon
and iron out any further details as we, like you, are looking
forward to a truly successful product launch.

Erica

This is a "send-them-a-rose" strategy. Rather than responding in
kind, Erica has smoothed the waters of dissention with kind words.
She could have told Tom that he is a fool or that he has his facts
wrong. She has every right to be angry about his decision to copy
the memo to Rob before giving her a chance to reply, but if Rob
knows Tom does these kinds of things, fighting with him won't help
Erica and would only bring her down a level in Rob's eyes. She took
the high ground, and usually that's the best ground to take. She can
work out any details, even let Tom get some anger off his chest
when they meet, but e-mail is not the way to do that. She's managed
to address what should be his main factual concern—advertising
went over budget and marketing might have to foot the bill. The
rest of his e-mail is full of attacks. Addressing them just breathes life
into them.

There are times, of course, when you do need to respond to
people in e-mail form in a way that lets them know that they're not
only wrong, but that you're not pleased either. The shot-over-their-
bow e-mail is of this sort. It sets things straight. Here too, however,
the high ground is best. If Erica could not speak with Rob first and
if she needed to reply in an e-mail that let Rob know her view, she
might have responded like this:

Tom: First let me respond to your key concern. Marketing will
not need to foot the bill for an advertising override. You may
recall last year that we expressed a similar concern when your
department had to go over budget. So, we understand your
concerns. Jill Miller, director of advertising here, suggested that

we meet sometime in the next week to discuss your concerns. We believe you'll find what we have to say reassuring and that we'll be able to continue working together as effectively as we have in the past.

Erica
Cc: Rob Milton

With this e-mail Erica has informed Rob and reminded Tom that advertising is not the only department that has gone over budget. Her tone is pleasant and professional. She lets Tom and Rob know that her boss has been apprised and that they're poised to work the issue out amicably. She took a small shot over Tom's bow by telling him that his department went over budget, but she doesn't aim the information at his jugular. She offers a solution meeting, and puts the ball in Tom's court. He can reply in a defensive manner, but Erica's professionalism limits his options. If he does insult her again, he'll make himself look the lesser person.

In some organizations, a confident attack is admired more than an amicable and professional response. If Erica knows that a pleasant e-mail will suggest weakness on her part, she could reply more assertively, as in the next example.

Tom: I've looked over the budget and there are two points that must be made. First, advertising is one of six departments that went over budget, something discussed at the meeting you missed last week. Second, at no time in the past has marketing picked up budget overrides for advertising, and we wouldn't expect that now either. If you would like to discuss this further, I suggest we meet before the end of the week.

Erica
Cc: Rob Milton

The tone of this e-mail conveys a don't-mess-with-me message. It's not accusatory or retaliatory. It states the facts, as Erica knows them. Suggesting a meeting may cause Tom to think twice before he replies. If he dumps further complaints into an e-mail after she's offered to meet and discuss the issues civilly, he risks making himself look petty and petulant.

E-mails, unlike conversation, are permanent and subject to considerable misinterpretation. It's wise to use them cautiously in politically delicate situations. You have to know what kinds of responses are respected where you work, and you need to know what matters most. Retaliation may feel like the best response to an accusatory e-mail, but give it a day. There may be a more productive road to take.

LIES AND BIG LIES

As Erica's last e-mail indicates, people do lie in business as they do elsewhere. Dishonesty, we've established, is frequent in human interaction. It ranges from the benign white lie to outright deceptions masking ulterior motives. Benign deception often involves telling half-truths to protect or avoid offending another person. These types of lies are used frequently in social situations to help maintain calm. People who engage in ulterior motive deception, however, often hope to benefit at someone else's expense. All forms of deception are lies, in the strictest sense of the word, but some are socially acceptable—even necessary—whereas others are strategically employed to advance a goal.

When someone important leaves the company, a memo may be circulated that mentions he or she left to spend more time with family or seek opportunities in another field. In many cases, though, the person is leaving because of a falling out with someone higher-up. The phrase "fake it until you make it" refers to the extensive amount of truth stretching many organizations expect. People learn to put on their "game faces" and "go with the flow." The late British prime minister Winston Churchill called such behavior "terminological inexactitude."[2] But just as "A rose by any other name would smell as sweet," a lie is a lie. Of course, some lies become so embedded in a system that they start to seem like truths.

I was invited to advise a financial institution as it recovered from revelations of corruption. In such circumstances, there is usually a lot of denial. This was especially the case here, however, because the organization had been perpetuating a culture of dishonesty. Its assessment indicated that concerns about upsetting the apple cart, so to speak, had become so embedded in the culture that people went out of their way to operate in a hear-no-evil, see-no-evil fashion. After a time, they even began to condone lies. It was all part of being a good team player. If everyone around you is living a lie, then it's not long before you find yourself living one too. People avoided taking responsibility for poor results. They blamed mistakes on others, and doing whatever pleased the boss became second nature. Everyone was guarded about what they said. Outspoken people were branded "complainers," "troublemakers," or "loose cannons" and were moved into out groups or moved out of the company altogether. Loyalty became an excuse for turning a blind eye, but it was fear of losing jobs that drove the truth underground. One day a person who'd had enough decided to blow the whistle. Accounting errors of significant magnitude were discovered, and the press had a feeding frenzy—one the company richly deserved. It had created its culture, lived in it, benefited from it, and eventually became victimized by it.

Given the prevalence of deception in human communication, it's important to learn how to detect it so you don't fail to see when you're surrounded by liars. One way is to recognize the disconnect that occurs between verbal and nonverbal expression. Nonverbal expert Paul Ekman explains and demonstrates how facial expressions can give away liars. His work provides a means of training oneself to detect lies, as I'll explain momentarily.[3] This skill is extremely important to the development of your red-flag warning system. It is not easily acquired, although Ekman has improved people's lie detection abilities in only one session. His work helps confirm my belief that those willing to put in the study and practice can develop political intuition.

When lies fail, it is usually because some nonverbal sign of emotion leaked. According to Ekman, the stronger the emotions involved in telling the lie and the greater their number, the more likely it is that leakage will occur. There are two primary ways to lie, he tells us: by concealing and by falsifying. When there is a choice, liars usually prefer concealing. Concealing is easier since there is no need to remember what you said. There are many ways to conceal: Claiming you forgot, didn't have the whole story, or intended to reveal information later are all types of excuses that people can easily stick to. Once a false statement has been made, however, a good deal of thought typically goes into preventing its discovery. Some people reject both concealment and falsifying in favor of misidentifying their feelings (e.g., describing anger as passion about the subject under discussion). There is also the option of "telling the truth with a twist" so that the victim doesn't believe it and doesn't question you. Exaggeration is an example of this type of lie. "Oh, sure, I went into the mailroom and read your mail. I do that every day. You caught me." Even if the liar does read mail, he covers himself by acting as if the accusation were so outlandish that it can't possibly be true. Yet he didn't deny reading the mail. Another dodging technique is the misdirected inference. Ekman refers to a humorous account by columnist Jon Carroll, which appeared in the *San Francisco Chronicle* in 1983:

> You are at the opening of your friend's art exhibition. You think the work is dreadful, but before you can sneak out your friend rushes over and asks you what you think. "Jerry," you say (assuming the artist in question is named Jerry), gazing deep into his eyes as though overcome by emotion, "Jerry, Jerry, Jerry." Maintain the clasp; maintain the eye contact. Ten times out of ten Jerry will finally break your grip, mumble a modest phrase or two, and move on. . . . There are variations. There's the high-tone artcrit third-person-invisible two-step, thus: "Jerry. *Jer-ry*. What can one

say?" Or the more deceptively low-key: "Jerry. Words fail me." Or the somewhat more ironic: "Jerry. Everyone, *every-one*, is talking about it."[4]

If Jerry were attuned to lies, he might have detected his friend's insincerity. But he would need to be sensitive to disconnects between verbal and nonverbal expression and his friend would have to be a typical liar—a detectable one. Most of us leak clues to our deception, which is just one of the reasons why lying is a bad policy. But because most of us are also less adept at detecting lies than we could be with a little training and practice, liars often get away with their transgressions.

People who are apprehensive about lying tend to leak clues more than their guiltless counterparts. Adept liars are often skillful actors, so detection is difficult. Liars, Ekman explains, manage their words and facial expressions to avoid detection. It's easier to manage words than facial expressions, so the leak is more likely to occur in the latter. But a truly good liar can control his or her facial expressions as well, so you also must be attentive to bodily clues. The body leaks clues to lies all the time, but because we're so used to listening to words and watching faces, most of us miss such clues. When emotions are strong, even practiced liars have difficulty keeping their voices, bodies, word choices, and speed of expression from revealing the absence of truth. The only way to detect practiced liars is to watch for how they leak clues of their deceit through what Ekman terms "emblems," "illustrators," and "manipulators."

Emblems are actions with very precise meanings known to almost everyone within a culture group, such as a wave or the raising of the middle finger in the United States. Emblems can, therefore, be used in place of words. Sometimes when liars are trying to hide their true feelings with contrived words, the inadvertent use of an emblem or part of one gives them away. Head nods and shakes are emblems. Emblematic slips occur when the person speaking is busy concentrating on the lie and, as a result, can't control everything else. For example, an inadvertent roll of the eyes or a twiddling of thumbs during a conversation can reveal boredom, even when the speaker feigns excitement.

Illustrators emphasize what is being said in speech. Our hands do a good deal of illustrating as we speak. Waving a fist while expressing anger or frustration, finger-snapping while searching for a word, looking upward as if the word were floating in the air and ready to be snatched—these gestures are illustrators. People tend to illustrate more when they are furious, horrified, agitated, distressed, or excited. When people use fewer illustrators than usual, they may be lying. People also use fewer illustrators when they are having trouble deciding what to say. If you can't just say what you're thinking, the theory goes, then you must be making up at least part of it. To spot lying by observing illustrators, you need to know the speaker rather well so you can see if he or she is doing something different. Perhaps your boss walks back and forth when he talks but does less of this when he lies. Or maybe he looks right at you when telling the truth, but off to the side when lying. Some people scratch the backs of their heads, move their tongue against their cheeks, or tap with their pens when lying. Card players call this kind of giveaway a "tell." Over time and with close observation, almost anyone's tells will become evident.

Manipulators are body movements that are often considered clues to the existence of deceit, but Ekman warns against making hasty judgments here. They include "all those movements in which one part of the body grooms, massages, rubs, holds, pinches, picks, scratches or otherwise manipulates another body part."[5] We learn politely to ignore such bodily grooming—we consider such fidgeting as a sign of nervousness. In fact, most of them are merely habits, not indicators of lying. Because practiced liars generally are aware that manipulators suggest they're lying, they squelch them. With these people, the *absence* of a manipulator may be a better clue of lying than its presence.

Another indicator of lying (or at least the absence of the whole truth) are "microexpressions." Such expressions flash across the face in less than a quarter of a second, leaking concealed emotions to those with a trained eye. They occur when people become aware that emotional expressions are about to give away their actual feelings and attempt to squelch the expression and replace it with another. A forced smile is squelched emotion, but it cannot hide signs of emotion that pop up in other parts of the face, such as in the eyes. When the smile doesn't match the rest of the face, most people can detect that true emotions are not being expressed. Crooked expressions, where facial actions are slightly stronger on one side of the face than the other, are another example. Expressions held longer than is typical for the individual or in a particular culture also can indicate masked emotions. So too can expressions that are too brief in duration. Temporal placement of an expression can also be telling. Nonverbal expressions of anger that appear only *after* statements like "I'm fed up with your behavior" are more likely to be false than if the anger appears at the start of, or even a moment before, such words.

Obviously, there is a great deal to learn about expressions and body language if you're going to use them to detect deceit. To become confident about reading such clues, it's important to familiarize yourself with the way your coworkers communicate when they're being truthful and when they're not. One person's nervous twitch may be a strong indicator of lying in another. If you're going to play in the big leagues of politics, you also need to know when people are holding back information and when they're out-and-out lying to you. The benefits to be derived from learning how to read beyond the mere content of words and into their true meaning are worth every ounce of effort required. If you choose to skip learning this aspect of political intuition, you'll be giving a lot of unsavory people a very significant advantage.

EMPATHY

Intuition not only involves reading people's expressions and in between the lines of what they say, but also getting into their minds to see and feel things as they do. Psychologist Carl Rogers defined empathy as "entering the private perceptual world of the other and becoming thoroughly at home in it. It involves being sensitive, moment to moment, to the changing felt meanings which flow in this other person."[6] This is a tall order, especially in today's fast-paced world. "Empathy" comes from the Greek word *empatheia*, which means "an active appreciation of another person's emotional experience." Unlike sympathy, which involves feeling sorrow or concern for someone, empathy requires a journey beyond our own thinking into the mental and emotional processes of others. It comes more naturally to some people than to others. Yet like other components of intuition, empathy can be learned and improved. Once again, the primary ingredient is openness accompanied by a penchant for observation.

The political advantage to those who can empathize effectively is a deep understanding of how another person thinks and feels. "If I were her, how would I feel right now?" is a question that requires stepping outside of your own mental world. If you've been doing this most of your lifetime, you have an advantage, unless you simply can't be empathic without wearing yourself out or losing sight of your objective.

POLITICAL ADVANTAGE #2

Developing empathy for the benefit of political advantage starts with an interest in other people, what they have to say and how they think and feel.

Empathy is not about judging people; it's about exploring their behavior. We suspend the very human tendency to pass judgment on others when we attempt to get to know a person through empathy. We ask questions and observe behaviors, and an understanding emerges that could not be derived in the presence of premature assumptions. After we check our understanding for accuracy, it then becomes the bridge from one person to another. It affords a connection that enables both people to predict the other's behaviors. In this way, empathy provides a two-part advantage—one of understanding why another person sees an issue as he or she does and another of being able to predict what that person is likely to do next.

High-level political skill requires empathy. Nothing less will do. Much of politics at this level involves astute persuasion, and, as I discuss in Chapter 5, persuasion is about encouraging another person to choose to think or act in your preferred manner. You can't do this effectively if you don't know how the other person thinks and feels about an issue. Only by visiting others' mental worlds can you gather the necessary information to bring them closer to you.

You can start improving your empathy skills right away. For example, tomorrow try leaving the safety of your assumptions and venturing into the minds of those around you. Find out what makes them tick. Do one or more of the following:

- Listen and learn. Become one of those rare people who have a deep interest in what people have to say, who wants to know what really makes others tick.
- Ask questions you've neglected to ask in the past.
- Probe into the details of someone's perceptions. Note that doing this is extraordinarily difficult.
- Don't judge or infer, even though you've become trained to do so.

Spend an entire morning practicing your empathy skills. Pick a few key people and really pay attention to them. This experience is likely to be enlightening, one that begins to transform you into a more effective politician. After all, being empathic isn't only admirable; it's absolutely critical.

FINDING THE INSIDE TRACK

Learning how other people think is a lot easier when you're on "the inside track." When you are, access to information from those higher up the organizational ladder is much more readily available. Once you prove that you are a trustworthy handler of information, you'll find yourself on this track. Of course, getting to this point is not easy. In order to work your way in to the inside track, you have to know how to be at the right places at the right times doing the right things. Most organizations have these inside tracks, but few make them easy to find.

In order to become politically intuitive, you need to have connections with people who receive insider information. You can't read the tea leaves if they won't even invite you to tea. So, the first important step is to become connected to at least one person who seems to know how your company works. Find a reason to talk with this person. An IBM senior executive told me that he visits an important person once a day. But he's careful not to waste their time. He asks questions that help with projects he's working on. He insists that he wouldn't be where he is today if he hadn't forced himself to do this.

Many of us are more comfortable achieving competence than connectedness. But competence alone is insufficient. Getting connected with people in the know is a necessary secret to success in most organizations. You don't have to be a star player in the connection game; just be sure you're not out of the loop. If you seem to be the last to hear about upcoming changes, if you find yourself constantly caught unaware, then likely you're not connected to the right people. Reevaluate your network. Does it need an insider or two—people you can do a favor for from time to time in exchange for valuable information? Perhaps you have a skill that this person needs. Why not offer to help with an important project? Find out where you might be able to provide assistance and indicate your willingness to do so.

In one of my interviews, a senior VP of a large U.S. information technology company told me how one of the people she was mentoring failed to take her advice about making connections. For example, this young woman refused to attend a company picnic where all the senior executives would be playing baseball, meeting, and talking casually with junior people. The senior VP explained that some of her success had come from her participation at this yearly function and others like it. "I told her several times that such social events are every bit as important as what she does at work. She just didn't agree. She had other demands on her time and couldn't see her way through to coming to the picnic for even a while. A truly bad move around here." Much to her surprise, the young woman was not promoted during the next round. Her technical competence was never questioned, but no one really knew her; few had even heard of her. After that letdown, she attended more social events and began connecting with people, but she had to learn the hard way.

Being on the inside track not only helps you predict what is about to happen, but also lets you know how and when to respond. Timing is critical in politics, as is the intensity of your responses. When should you go to the mat on an issue? Is there another way to achieve your goals that doesn't require a confrontation? Some issues are best left for another day or are best responded to in a less intense way than another person might expect. Again, a kind of intuition is helpful here, the kind based on your observations of successful people in your organization—when they've pushed hard to obtain something and when they've held back. In the next chapter I'll discuss how to develop insight into this kind of knowledge. Political intuition provides the red-flag alert, while insight provides creative ways to address the situations you've identified as a result of your intuition, connections with insiders, or emergence as an insider yourself.

Political intuition operates like other forms of intuition. The farmer who senses it's time to bring in the hay, the race-car driver who seems to instinctively avoid an accident, the fisherman who knows when to head back to port, the batter who can read a pitch the instant it leaves the pitcher's hand, and the intuitive politician all share an ability to read cues others miss or ignore. It isn't instinct that sets them apart, but rather the experience they've learned to put to use in very effective ways. Hardly anyone hits a home run their first time at bat, and it's a rare city person who can determine when to bring in the hay or head for shore. These kinds of knowledge come from observing and learning. The same is true of political intuition. Developing a political advantage at work means knowing where to find the knowledge you need to become intuitive. It calls for a sharpening of observations and an openness to information previously blocked by faulty assumptions.

Most human behavior is influenced by norms or rules. If you don't know what to expect from people, how can you know when they step beyond those norms? If you don't know the rules, how can you know when you're breaking them? The answer is simple: You can't. But by observing and learning from others, you can learn the rules. Ask yourself the following questions to see how much you know about your organization.

- In your organization, who talks to whom and when?
- Who talks first, for how long? What are their agendas?
- Who are the insiders?
- What are their views and what stories do they share about the organization?
- How do the people around you get things done?
- What are their motives and attitudes toward work issues?
- Whose side are they on—and is it yours?
- What inconsistencies have they demonstrated in their words and behaviors?
- What types of behaviors are rewarded and by whom?
- What organizational fictions are passed around, and what happens to people who buy into them?
- Your company probably has an inside track. Are you on it?

Answering these questions will help you take strong steps forward in your development of political intuition. They will put you in touch with what really goes on in your organization. In time, the questions will come to mind naturally, and their answers will help you interpret current conditions and predict future ones. Very little slips by politically intuitive people who approach situations with these kinds of questions on their minds. In the next chapter, I'll explain what these advantaged people do with this knowledge.

CHAPTER THREE

POLITICAL INSIGHT

INTUITION MAY BE indispensable to political acumen, but it only provides a sense of what is about to happen. Knowing what to do once you have this sense calls for a different skill: political insight.

As we discussed, people tend to be lazy information processors. The choices we make usually lead to rather routine, shallow, or trivial outcomes. When people stretch beyond the mundane, when we think creatively, the result is often unusual, profound, and important. Such outcomes are the products of insight. Insightful ideas are ones that seem to get to the core of an issue in novel, interesting ways.[1] Skillful politicians don't settle for simplistic responses to problems when the potential outcomes could have significant effects on their futures. They don't allow themselves to slip into old patterns of thinking. They stretch themselves to identify responses that are beyond the norm.

Skillful politicians train themselves to think outside the box, to use common business vernacular. When confronted by a problem, like most people, they begin the process of finding a solution. At some point during the search, however, when simple solutions seem inadequate, insightful people begin to think creatively. They bring together ideas that others might see as disparate or apply what they learned from an entirely different situation to the current problem. Often these insights appear to onlookers to come from out of the blue. In reality they are usually the product of hard work and research followed by a period of reflection during which insightful people piece together what they've learned in novel ways. In other words, insight, like creativity, is 99 percent perspiration and 1 percent inspiration.

When people say that they just can't think as fast as insightful people, they are selling themselves short. Speed is not the issue. Receptivity to novel ways of thinking and the development of a kind of personal brainstorming in the search for a solution are the keys to insightfulness. A willingness to let the subconscious mind inform the conscious is critical. Researchers believe that insight depends on chance combinations of thought processes below the threshold of awareness.[2] Most insight experts believe that the mind can subconsciously transform ideas in ways that enable "Aha!" experiences once they are brought to the conscious level and combined with more conscious thought. Insightful people possess an ability that allows the subconscious to cue the conscious mind to think in novel ways. Doing this may seem a tall order, but it is not beyond the grasp of people willing to experiment, learn, and occasionally fail.

A comforting thought is that insight does not occur in isolation. It is often brought on by social interaction. Sir Isaac Newton once said, "If I have seen further than others, it is because I have stood on the shoulders of giants." He attributed much of his remarkable success as a scientist to having learned from work done by other people. He was a synthesist, capable of drawing on the work of great minds like Johannes Kepler, Copernicus, and Galileo. From his considerations of their work and his own creative genius, he was able to develop his "law of gravitation," which stated that the force generated between two masses is proportional to their masses and inversely proportional to the square of their separation. His contributions to mathematics also were based on the works of other great thinkers.

So it isn't as if you need to come up with all the ingredients of an insight yourself. Most insights are in part derived from the thoughts of others. If you are a good observer, you're partway there.

By reading this book, you are learning from the insights of the successful people I've interviewed over two decades. Here are just a few tactics that can facilitate your development of insightfulness:

- Read biographies for insights.
- Observe how more savvy persons communicate at meetings.
- Pay attention to how their memos read.
- Notice how they relate to people.
- Understand how they use power and formulate connections.

AN INSIGHTFUL EXCHANGE

Insightful people take in information from others in a manner that is unique. They do not immediately criticize or rebut what they hear. Instead, they tend to absorb, assess, and then synthesize the information they receive. Often this synthesis helps them see the problem differently, results in a novel solution, or both. I observed two managers who were unable to get along with each other no matter how much each of them tried. Yet they had to work together. She thought his inability to make decisions, fear of the unknown, and desire for complete consensus was a sluggish way to deal with issues she wanted to resolve swiftly to avoid giving the competition the upper hand. He considered her brash, demanding, and unwilling to compromise. After a leadership styles session, both of them filled out a style inventory. Their scores were nearly opposite. "He scored as an amicable, supportive leader and I as an aggressive, commanding type," the female manager explained. "Looking at our scores, it occurred to me that we weren't so different in what we wanted as we were in our styles of going about getting it. I realized then that our problem was not one of personalities which are permanent. Style is something you can work on." Her eyes were wide when she told me this, as if she'd uncovered a deep secret. Once they discussed their style differences, they began to work more ef-

A SMART BET

Jack Gallaway, chairman of Isle of Capri Casinos, came up with a new way of accomplishing his objectives when faced with a boss who did not see things his way.

> While president of the Tropicana in Las Vegas, working for Ramada Corporation, I wanted to build a second large hotel tower. Ramada had no money and was barely limping along, and I was told to not even consider the expansion. Things were so tough they wouldn't even give me the money to work on the concept designs. . . . I decided to push ahead and see what I could do without spending any money. I hooked up with the president of the Mardian Group in Phoenix who was in the process of building the Thomas and Mack Stadium in Las Vegas, and in return for being on the inside should the project get the go-ahead, his firm did the complete concept drawings and model for free, work that at that time was worth over $100,000. It got me what I needed, plus some inevitable corporate criticism for being a loose cannon. Six months later, though, I was able to go to the board when we had more money to get approval to move ahead. That hotel expansion was the first of the new wave of hotel rooms in Las Vegas.

Gallaway's solution was creative if not insightful. He discovered a way to do what he wanted to do without fighting those higher up the ladder—and without spending any money. Insightful thinking requires this kind of stretching of the mind, finding creative ways to achieve goals.

fectively with each other because they'd defined a common problem rather than thinking of each other as *the* problem. They joked about their styles—she'd tell him he was dragging his feet and he'd comment about domineering leaders. "We were able to work together," she explained. "It wasn't perfect, but at least we had reasons for the obstacles we had been attributing to personality flaws and could even joke about style differences, which cleared the air."

When confronted by a political problem, insightful people have an advantage. They can reconstruct their goals or keep their original goals while coming up with novel means of achieving them. When everyone else is expecting them to take one approach, the politically skilled often take another because they are versatile in their thinking. They make themselves unpredictable because they don't allow themselves to slip into limited reasoning habits. Instead, just when a situation seems difficult or even impossible, they present a way of looking at the problem that opens up a number of previously unforeseen options.

A senior technology executive from an aerospace company shared with me how he managed to bring a difficult negotiation to a positive close by rethinking his company's goals. His company had no Japanese competitors in Japan prior to the 1990s, but by the mid-1990s, his company's market share had diminished to a critical point. It had either to strike a partnership deal of some sort with a Japanese competitor or withdraw from the Japanese market.

Negotiations with a targeted Japanese competitor dragged on for a year and a half. The Japanese competitor acknowledged that it too needed the deal because the company also was losing money and needed the Americans' technology. But personalities stood in the way.

The negotiation session in Osaka was bogged down, with everyone rehashing the same old positions. Everyone was getting irritated. The recalcitrant Japanese negotiator, whom no one on the Japanese team would dare overrule, feared that the Americans would take advantage of his company and withhold their most important technology. In this sense, he saw them as the enemy rather than as a partner. The American technology executive realized this and decided to revise his Japanese counterpart's sense of distrust. It would take a bold step. He decided to focus on his company's original goal and forget about winning and losing. With the assumption that the negotiations ultimately would lead to a joint venture agreement, the executive proposed combining respective research and development efforts immediately so as not to lose precious time. He proposed transferring one or two key personnel to the Japanese R&D lab, defining the new product they'd jointly develop for the Japanese market, and launching the development. The executive noted, "Since this offer was made without consulting my team, much less my boss, the company president, it could have been political suicide, especially, because my coleader of our team is a political enemy. But instead the move proved to be an insightful decision because I took into consideration all conditions impinging on action and then removed the ones that were obstacles. I addressed the concerns of key stakeholders, ourselves included, but especially those of the Japanese negotiator who was beginning to dig in his heels. My offer stunned the Japanese. I had just given him everything he could want. He happily agreed. Six months later we hammered out the final joint venture agreement. Today the joint venture still exists and is successful in Japan. If we'd continued to focus on winning, rather than our goal of cooperation, we would have had an entirely different ending."

Flexibility in thinking is especially important in highly and pathologically political environments. Much of what goes on in these types of organizations involves less than up-front behavior. If you're predictable in highly political organizations or divisions or during negotiations, you're a sitting duck. People will soon know what gets you upset, what will lead you to do something rash, and how to sabotage your career, if they have it in their minds to do so. Survival in highly politicized arenas requires versatility of action — an extensive repertoire of possible responses to a wide variety of potential situations. Ask yourself how you'd respond in the following brief scenarios. Do you have multiple options that are not politically dangerous?

• You've learned that a project report that you worked on was given to the senior VP of your division prior to your approval of the final draft. Your name was not included on the cover page or anywhere on the report. It had been given to the senior VP by Dan, a project team member who frequently disparages your ideas in public but is not above using them in reports and claiming them as his own.

• You're the senior VP of marketing at your company. A new CEO has just arrived. Others at your level are making a point of going to his office to meet him. This feels a bit obsequious to you, yet it is typical in this company's highly political environment. Should you wait until the CEO settles in or asks to meet you? Or is it essential that you go to the CEO?

• Contrary to company rules, your boss is dating one of your female colleagues. She dislikes you. You believe she has told him negative things about you because he's been distant toward you since they began their relationship. A few things he said have confirmed your suspicion. At a team meeting, he made a comment about you being closed-minded and territorial, the same words she once used to describe you. You're very uncomfortable at work now. She seems almost smugly confident around you, as if she knows she has an advantage.

These scenarios can be dealt with in a variety of insightful ways. Be sure to consider carefully what matters most to you in each case.

• What should your *front-burner* issue(s) be? Establish and prioritize goals. Don't allow yourself to be easily satisfied with your choice. Make sure it's the largest issue for you. For example, in the final scenario, what exactly do you want to accomplish? Is it enough for the boss to know that you're concerned about what he is being told about you? Do you want some assurance that he will evaluate you fairly?

- Perhaps she hasn't disparaged you. Try some probing questions to test your assumptions.

- Watch for body language and facial expressions; you may gain more information there than in the other person's words.

- If, in the final scenario, your boss denies that your colleague has said anything negative about you, what are your options? What if he claims that you're exaggerating or that he is offended that you'd suggest that he'd take sides in such a manner? What is the political downside of that?

- Can you risk a confrontation? Or should you take a more indirect approach?

- Whose toes are likely to be stepped on, whose self-image threatened with each potential response?

- What do you stand to lose, what will you gain, and can you live with a negative result?

These are the kinds of questions that should go into any political decision. Diving in without considering the downside is too risky. In most political situations, you need to consider whether you should act now or take some time to make sure you're right. Do you have a good course of action? Do you have a mentor you can trust or a politically savvy peer? Ask for his or her opinion. Another perspective can be invaluable. Remember, insightful responses are rarely developed in isolation. The best ones are often developed in the company of other insightful people.

HOW TO DEVELOP VERSATILITY

One of the best ways I've seen to become a more versatile thinker is what author Tony Buzan calls "mind mapping." Mind mapping, a topic on which Buzan has written several books, is a technique for expanding thought, for encouraging insights. As I've noted, insights are not wisdom formed out of ether, but rather are the result of studying a problem, listening to the opinions of others, and achieving a synthesis. Therefore, any exercise that helps to move the mind away from old habits may be useful in eliciting insights. Mind mapping is one such exercise.

When speaking publicly, Buzan often asks people to list the uses of a paper clip. Most people come up with four or five uses. Then he asks them to list things you *can't* do with a paper clip. Those lists tend to be much longer. Why? Buzan asks. Is it because there are more things you can't do with a paper clip than things you can do? Or is it because by the time the second question is asked, your mind already has had some practice thinking beyond the obvious? It is freed from some of its constraints and allowing you to come up with more options. Buzan explains that we use so little of our minds during much of each day that we could benefit considerably from stretching them. The following mind maps pertain to the scenarios I raised earlier. The first one has to do with the new CEO case described on page 44. Here are a number of possible choices of how to introduce yourself to the new CEO.

As in most first-draft mind maps, some of the options are not as good as others. In fact, the way to use mind maps is to identify a number of potential options and then to omit ones that seem too risky or ill-advised in the political climate in which you work. For example, take the new CEO case. Introducing yourself to the CEO too soon could seem too aggressive. On the other hand, if you wait too long, you run the risk of appearing indifferent. Attempts to run

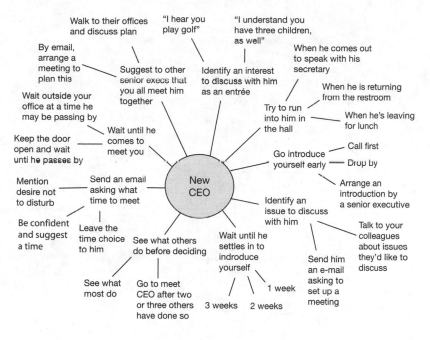

into him in the halls might get his attention, but they might also look contrived—or even ridiculous. A mind map can help you come up with a host of solutions, many of which you'll decide to eliminate in favor of better ones. In this case, try identifying a real issue to discuss with him and asking him to set up a meeting, or learn a little about him to see if you have anything in common. Of course, there are pros and cons to most of the options in the mind map, and there are certainly others that you can add. But no matter how your mind map looks, it can be very effective in helping you better assess your options when making a decision.

The second mind map refers to the example about the worker whose name was left off the report. The same process of elimination and replacement should be used here.

Here again one question to ask is which of these options suit you. Then ask which ones are politically dangerous and which ones simply won't work in your division or organization. What are the pros and cons of each? In this case, you'd want to be sure you're not making a false assumption when concluding that Dan purposefully left your name off the report. After assuring yourself that you

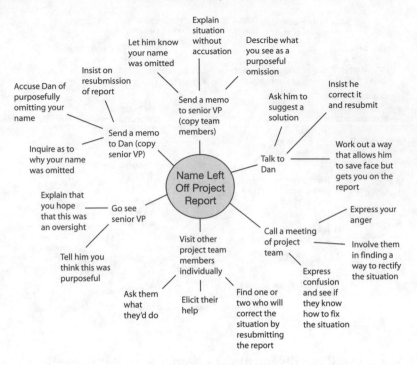

haven't assumed incorrectly, you'll want to assess the options you've identified and select one that has promise. When unsure, a good approach is a gradual one. You might go directly to Dan but, instead of blaming him or insisting that he rectify the situation, see if he comes up with an acceptable solution on his own. He might offer to send a memo copied to the senior VP that mentions the omission of your name and describes your extensive contribution to the project. Ask to see the memo before it is sent—showing you is the least he can do. If he refuses to do that, then another solution is advisable as he may have a trick up his sleeve.

You may not always have the time to draw mind maps, but it is important always to think in terms of multiple options or avenues. By doing so you can journey beyond the obvious choices, discover options you hadn't previously noticed, and make yourself less predictable. Skilled politicians approach potentially difficult situations looking for multiple options. Using Buzan's mind mapping as a practice device can help you to stretch beyond simplistic or habitual problem-solving techniques. Once you start working in this way—once you are no longer satisfied with your tired old problem-solving processes that have become second nature—you're likely to make significant progress toward more insightful solutions.

When preparing to enter a difficult politicized situation, it is possible to anticipate potential areas of disagreement. A mind map can help you anticipate these disagreements. Skilled negotiators think in such terms. If you write your mind maps down on paper, you can refer to them during negotiation sessions. Develop mind maps for each negotiation issue. See how well you do with the mini-case below, one I used in a training session for senior executives of an executive placement firm.

EXECUTIVE PLACEMENT CASE

Elise, one of the consultants in your branch, has been annoying you lately. Whenever you ask her to do something, she rushes off before you have a chance to complete your thoughts. You've been hearing rumors about her abruptness. Just last week you told her that she should spend more time on the telephone with the executive placement candidates. Her response was a casual "Okay," and off she went before you could stop her. You knew then that she'd probably just keep doing things the way she has been. Today, though, one of your best executive candidates requested a change in consultants. According to him, Elise has no time for questions. "She finds you a job, but she doesn't give you any background," he said. "If she has three minutes to give you, then you're doing well," he added.

When you attempted to speak with her about this request, she interrupted you. She said, "He's a pain. Good riddance is how I see it," and then, as she edged out of your office as she has so many times before, she said, "I've got to get back to my desk." Clearly she doesn't have much time for anybody. Yet, surprisingly, she is one of the more productive of your consultants. She is a hard worker and you'd rather not lose her, as it would affect the division's numbers and the CEO's view of your department's productivity. In fact, this is why you haven't confronted Elise yet.

The question is: Can you continue to allow her to be so abrupt with you and the candidates? Is continuing silence a more practical political move than confronting her? If you decide to confront the issue of her abruptness, how can you get her to sit still long enough to impress upon her that you want to see a change?

This mini-case presents many levels of complexity. And any case involving real people is going to be even more complex. This is why those who are political have an advantage. They know how to manage such complexity. They start by sorting out the important issues. What matters to them the most? Then they consider their options and the political upside and downside to each. They might then discuss their options with a trusted coworker, someone who is sensitive to the organization's and division's political culture and the people who work there. I've listed these steps next.

STEPS CHART

1. Identify your primary goals.
2. Pick the goals most pressing or most important to you.
3. Develop a set of options (perhaps using a mind map approach).
4. Go over each option, considering the political upsides and downsides.
5. Consider whether you might wait to respond (if there are political downsides).
6. Discuss your options with a mentor or coach familiar with the political climate.
7. Revise your options.
8. Select the one that will most likely help you achieve your primary goals.

After step 8, the challenge is one of communication, which I will discuss in greater detail in Chapters 4 and 5. For now, try applying these preparation steps to the Executive Placement Case. What will you say to Elise, for example?

This multiple-option kind of thinking, whether you use a mind map or merely write down possible steps, encourages insightful solutions. There is always more than one way to solve any problem. Certainly circumstances can place restraints on some options, but stretching yourself to think in terms of multiple options often results in better outcomes. If your options seem too limited, perhaps a different goal or goals might be useful. In other words, think about something other than the obvious goal. Perhaps take an incremental approach.

For example, in the case where the boss was supposedly getting inaccurate information from an employee he is dating, one obvious goal might be to stop him from listening to her. This goal, however, is probably unattainable. If your boss likes this woman, and she decides to diss you, there is little you can do to stop them from talking about you. A more realistic goal might be to provide him with good reason to question the validity of her remarks about you. Given how he feels about her, I don't suggest disparaging her. Doing so is more likely to backfire. Instead, think of altering the situation gradually. Begin by having lunch with your boss. Stay away from the topic of his attraction to your colleague, and avoid saying anything negative about her. Instead, focus on goals he wants to achieve and how you can help him. Then work diligently toward those goals, letting him know when you've made progress. If this is working, continue on this course. He may begin to develop a better impression of you. Once you feel that you have gained his confidence, you've probably won. You've achieved a work-around. Even if you feel confident at that point, however, you probably wouldn't want to address the issue of your colleague, either directly or indirectly. If your boss were to take it wrong, the problem could quickly become acute. In business, some problems are chronic, and if you can work your way around them, you're doing well. It would be better to wait for another person to attempt the same sort of character assassination—

and sooner or later someone will—either with you or someone else. Then you could express to your boss your revulsion at such behavior and your incredulity at people who believe slander without checking the facts. That way you maintain complete deniability in regard to the boss's special friend, while helping to inoculate him against such behavior.

Persuading others is rarely a one-shot effort. Getting from point A to point C in the next diagram usually requires at least a step B, if not multiple steps between A and B and B and C.

Incremental Approach

A 1 2 3 4 B 1 2 3 4 C

In the scenario we just discussed, step A1 might be arranging to meet with your boss. Step A3 might be discussing ways you can be of more help to him. Step B could be the point at which you have gained his confidence, and B1 to B4 are steps you could take to change his thinking about gossip he may hear about you. Point C is where he develops a high regard for you and your work, and will no longer believe gossip to the contrary. How you define the incremental steps is naturally affected by the situation (e.g., how well you know this boss, your prior track record with him, how serious the relationship is with the woman who you believe gossips about you, and how open he is to your thoughts and opinions). When in doubt, use an incremental approach. You don't need to spread the steps over a long period of time. Just be sure to achieve your objective at each step along the way before moving to the next step.

WHEN INSIGHTFUL RESPONSES DON'T COME EASILY

At break times and after seminars, many people come up to me to say, "I just don't think fast on my feet." They marvel at people who seem to say exactly the right thing with little or no planning time. The truth is that, with rare exceptions, these people have planned their responses (at least to some extent). They may have kept in mind a similar previous situation that helped them respond to the current one. They may have expected that the challenge they're currently experiencing was likely to happen and prepared themselves. Alternatively, they may have a repertoire of responses for such occasions that they've developed over time. In any case, the responses of those who seem quick on their feet are likely not as spontaneous as they seem. When we watch a race-car driver, we may marvel at his or her quick reflexes, but we have not seen the extraordinary amount of study and practice preceding the feat. Indeed, some of the driver's success may be due to natural talent, as it is with some expert politicians. But even if you aren't politically insightful now, you can develop your ability using the same kind of study and practice that goes into any impressive performance.

POLITICAL ADVANTAGE #3

Because they devote the necessary time to study and practice, experienced politicians are rarely blindsided by the unexpected. They have asked themselves in advance what they might say should a delicate discussion go in any of a variety of directions.

The politically insightful use if-then scenarios to prepare: How should I respond if an unflattering comment is made about me? Perhaps the answer to that question is: I'll focus on the future, not on the past. If they attempt to draw me into blame placing, I'll say, "It would be easy for us to take a tit-for-tat approach here, but it won't get us where we want to go." If that's too wordy or lofty for you, another option is: "I'm sure neither of us is without regrets, but let's focus on our future rather than our past." Another example using Jack Gallaway's case: How should I respond if one of the senior executives learns that I've been going ahead with the plan they'd vetoed? A possible answer: I'll remind them that they'd merely said that the cost was prohibitive, not, to my recollection, that the project shouldn't be explored. I'll add, "So I found a no-cost way to make it happen." Gallaway might tell himself, "I won't get defensive. I'll suggest that they were a part in finding the solution given their receptivity to innovative ideas, and that I wouldn't have bothered if I thought otherwise."

All interactions have *choice points*, places where the course you're on can be altered, taking you down the right or the wrong path. You need to be ready for and attuned to choice points, in case changing (or continuing) course may be to your disadvantage. It's wise to consider possible choice points before meeting with someone to discuss a difficult issue or situation. Ask yourself: What might he or she say that could take me off course? During the meeting, be on the lookout for choice points where something they (or you) say may damage your chances of achieving your objective—or where something you (or they) say may improve your chances. Here's an example. The scenario I'll give involves two peers.

Alan heard that while he was ill, Stan replaced him at a meeting without alerting anyone else. Furthermore, a reliable source said that during the meeting, Stan disparaged a previous recommendation of Alan's. This is not the first time Stan has attempted to make Alan look bad. The week before, he'd laughed when Alan proposed an idea to their boss, then proceeded to describe all the ways the suggestion could go wrong.

What, Alan wonders, can he do? Angrily demand an apology? Complain about Stan's slippery tactics? Or (after doing the necessary groundwork) tell Stan that his tactic backfired and the project team is talking about what a fool he made of himself—a kind of touché? That might give Stan something to think about!

The good thing here is that Alan is thinking in terms of multiple options. Here's the downside, though: He's not checking his assumptions. He hasn't planned to ask Stan any questions. Nor has he considered how Stan's reply will affect his next move. Essentially, Alan has not prepared himself adequately. Because he's failed to develop his strategy sufficiently, the conversation might very well proceed something like this:

Alan: Stan, I need to talk to you.

Stan: I'm kind of busy right now.

Alan: This can't wait.

Stan: Judging from how red your face is, I'd say you're right. You look like you're about to have a heart attack.

Alan: I heard about the little game you played the other day.

Stan: The what?

Alan: You don't fool anyone. You attended the project meeting without checking with anyone, and then you took the opportunity to try and make me look bad.

Stan: Whoa! Slow down here. I didn't make you look bad; you did that to yourself. All I did was to save you from making a big mistake by showing them what would happen if they acted on your suggestion.

Alan: You're a moron.

Stan: And that's supposed to be an intelligent remark?

Alan: Stay away from my assignments.

In my previous book, *The Secret Handshake*, I introduced four political styles, the most covert and often manipulative one being the maneuverer. People with this political style look for ulterior motives in others, have little regard for sanctioned rules, and rely largely on subliminal politics. Maneuverers are smooth operators. Unlike purists, who believe in getting ahead by hard work, decline to participate in politics, and rely largely on sanctioned rules to get things done, maneuverers play fair only when it is to their advantage. Team players are more like purists than maneuverers, but are willing to participate in politics of the positive type in order to advance group goals. Finally, street fighters are not inhibited about using politics to advance their goals and are more likely than purists and team players to use subliminal and somewhat negative forms of politics to achieve their goals. They are masters of the cut and thrust of business, although they are not as willing as maneuverers are to use people and events to their advantage no matter the ethical cost.[3]

Stan shows all the signs of a maneuverer political style. He's not to be trusted. Alan appears to be more of a purist or team player. He's clearly no street fighter—if he was, he would have been more strategic in his approach. But the problem goes much deeper than Alan's style. He doesn't seem to know what he wants in terms of goals or remedies. Does he want to persuade Stan to stop sabotaging him? Threaten and humiliate him? Focus on one issue or establish that there's a pattern? What did he accomplish with Stan? Nothing, really. He didn't ask questions that would have helped him determine whether Stan had *purposely* undermined him. "What happened at the project meeting the other day?" is an open-ended question that would have provided him with some needed information. If the preceding conversation had taken place, Stan could easily tell their boss that Alan has accused him of treachery without even knowing what actually happened. If so, Alan set himself up for premature defeat. Instead of launching a frontal assault, he could have operated more incrementally. Here's how he might have proceeded.

Alan: Stan, I need your help with something.

Stan: I'm kind of busy right now.

Alan: I just have a question about last week's staff meeting.

Stan: Since you were sick, I thought it would be helpful if I filled in for you.

Alan: When you'd like to take my place at a meeting, I would like to know about it in advance. That way I can give you some background information first.

Stan: That's a fair point. *(Goes back to work.)*

Alan: Also, some things got back to me that might not be accurate, and I wanted to check with you. What did you say about the suggestion I made last week?

Stan: What did you hear?

Alan: Why don't you just tell me what you said?

Stan: Well, I can't give you chapter and verse, but I just made some suggestions for improvement.

Alan: Such as?

Stan: All I did was to save you from making a big mistake by showing them what would happen if they acted on your suggestion.

Alan: Again, you could have talked about it with me beforehand.

Stan: You were sick.

Alan: I have a phone. You can always call me, just as I would call you if something like this came up.

Stan: I'm not good at hand-holding. I saw a problem and fixed it.

Alan: Next time you see a problem that has to do with me, let's fix it together so neither of us has to get his back up or feel the need to reciprocate in kind.

Stan: Okay, Alan. I get it. Fair enough.

Here Alan's goals were to get information directly from Stan, to show Stan the error of his ways, and then, in the face of resistance, to identify a direction they could both take and accompany it with a warning that doing otherwise might force Alan to retaliate in kind. This last subtle pressure was in response to Stan's "hand-holding" comment, which dismissed Alan's first attempt at a mutual solution. Rather than react with anger, Alan proposed teamwork again, this time by indicating that this course would help Stan avoid making Alan into an enemy. Some people might be uncomfortable with the directness of Alan's comment about reciprocating in kind, but what Stan did was devious, and he may need to be shown clearly that such behavior in the future won't pass without some redress.

Anger tends to make people act more quickly than they should. Political ingenuity calls for considered responses that begin with an identification of the most important goals and move through multiple steps to achieve them.

NURTURING YOUR INSIGHTFULNESS

The process of becoming more insightful not only requires you to ask yourself questions and consider multiple options like the ones I've discussed, but also to recognize whether you've come to rely on certain problem-solving patterns. Until you identify the limiting cognitive ruts you've already fallen into, you'll never expand your thinking. To begin your personal assessment, you might ask people who know you well to describe how you tend to solve problems. Ask for some examples. Just be ready for some information you've successfully avoided hearing for some time. Then take what you've learned and try to approach problem solving differently. Be flexible when redefining an important goal or developing new ways of reaching a goal.

It's important to remember that every situation is multidimensional, meaning that it can be seen from a variety of vantage points, each providing a different view of the same thing. Experienced politicians keep this fact in mind, unlike political novices, who may know in theory that every situation can be seen from many sides, but who fail to take this fact into consideration when formulating a strategy. Political novices are myopic; they see only their own perspective.

POLITICAL ADVANTAGE #4

Of all the skills important to the development of political intelligence or ingenuity, the ability to see things as others do is paramount.

It's important to learn how to make sense of events and conditions as people important to your future make sense of them. Reasoning, after all, is about making sense of what occurs around us. Each of us does this somewhat differently no matter how similar our backgrounds or interests. *The primary job of any politician, whether in business or government, is to expand on his or her view of a signif-*

icant event or project in an effort to find the place where many points of view converge.

Learning how you solve problems should allow you to see whether your perceptions differ from people important to your progress. Do you see problems from only one vantage point? Or do you seek a point of convergence (or preferably a zone of convergence) between you and your coworkers? Are you fully aware not only of what they think but also of *how* they think? For most of us most of the time, the answer is no. There's usually so much going on around us that examining our own ways of making sense of situations and comparing them to those of others seems a luxury. Yet such examinations lead to advancement in political acumen—the kind that allows two people to talk with instead of past each other.

FRAMING

Another way to think about aligning one way of thinking with another is in terms of framing. Framing is an important strategy in persuasion. It refers to the manner in which people position themselves and their surroundings. A *framing effect* happens in communication when a speaker defines a situation in a particular way in an attempt to persuade those listening to accept his or her point of view. Often frames are metaphors, images or words effectively used to create impressions.[4] When the 1994 Northridge, California, earthquake drove my husband, three children, and me from our home, I looked at the terrified faces of my children, paused, took a breath, smiled, and said with contrived elation, "Aren't we having an adventure?" Their small faces relaxed into smiles. They had accepted my frame. Soon one child was fast asleep in a spared neighbor's intact living room, where we huddled waiting for the aftershocks to subside. The other two followed suit. The frame allowed them to categorize their experience as relaxed rather than fearful. Framing works in this way.

Why will we pay more for a drink in a hotel restaurant than we would for the same drink at a fast-food restaurant? It's the same beverage, but due to the hotel's atmosphere, we accept that drinks must necessarily cost more—perhaps far more than any cost-based comparison would justify. The décor is a form of framing; it conveys information that influences us to accept paying more or less for the same item. Similarly, politicians know how to organize information in a way that influences decision makers during negotiations. Skilled negotiators often frame their preferred options in terms of gains, a frame that influences others to accept those options. They also tend to frame options they do not prefer as losses.

Framing involves presenting key issues in ways that will elicit the responses you desire from other people. For example, a negotiator might describe a difficult negotiation as an opportunity for us to find the common ground or a chance for us to make a good working relationship a great one. What one person describes as a fight can be reframed by another as a disagreement on issues, thereby making the interaction less personal. A person who seems stubborn to some may appear determined or persistent to others. Simply by framing the same behavior differently, very different outcomes can result. A skillful politician can affect the course of events by carefully framing situations to favor his or her goals. Effective framing allows you to guide the unfolding of events instead of being managed by the frames of others.

Most people don't realize that frames guide what they think about and do in situations all day long. A conversation between close friends, for example, is very different from one between acquaintances. One person's learning experience is what another might consider a failure. We are inclined to deal more enthusiastically with challenges than with problems. Fairness is for many people a frame by which they measure life's events. But in business, cry "Unfair!" when a cost-cutting hotshot is promoted over a more qualified candidate, and you may learn that the most important frame in your organization is profitability.

Often framing is a cooperative endeavor rather than something contrived by one person and imposed on others. Sociologist Erving Goffman described "focused interactions" as instances when people openly join together to sustain a single common focus of concern. When people play games, for example, they know that certain types of unsportsmanlike or must-win displays are unacceptable. After all, it's just a game. When people share a definition of a situation, certain types of actions become required, others prohibited, and still others irrelevant. A frame borders the interaction and broadly defines what should and should not be said or done.[5]

Think about it. Most days you'll know by what type of conversation or activity you're participating in what behaviors are acceptable or desirable. Cocktail parties encourage certain types of behavior that may not be appropriate in team meetings, and vice versa. Once you begin to think in terms of frames, it's easy to see how you can use them to affect people's actions. A fight is different from a debate. A confidential conversation is different from a public discussion, and a boss-employee interaction has different rules from those between peers.

Insight may lead to novel ways of looking at issues or situations, but it is framing that will help you express your ideas. For example, politics itself can be and often is viewed as destructive to organizations. When this perspective is allowed to take root, people become victims, rather than managers, of politics. A manager who decides, however, to make sense of politics might decide to view it as a natural way for competitive people to behave. This fact-of-life frame allows the manager to expect politics instead of being shocked and appalled by it. It's the manager's first step in becoming able to manage politics.

Insights and frames are ways of reorganizing perceptions. As I've explained before, insights usually emerge after considerable study of a problem. Frames are used to set parameters on a situation and to convince others of which actions are reasonable and which are unreasonable.

Insights can be converted to frames to facilitate expression. For example, if a manager is faced with a significant problem but after careful study and a chance to step back and think has the insight to see that his "problem" is actually an advantage, he might convey this new view to his boss using a frame. He might explain that the obstacle they fear most, perhaps competition, is actually the incentive they need to drive them to greater success. Rather than dread the competition, the manager might say, we should welcome and even encourage it—if we are up to the challenge. Fear, he might add, makes us cautious; competition makes us risk takers—and only the risk-taking results in impressive success.

I coached a female senior manager in Los Angeles who considered herself very pragmatic but also unskilled in politics. She operated from a frame of "We're all in this together. We're a team and we should all help each other succeed." She encouraged success and rewarded it. So she was understandably disappointed when people working for her spread false gossip, misinformed each other, hoarded information, and engaged in petty turf wars. She had a political purist frame, but her environment was competitive. People produced or they were gone, no matter how hard she might try to retain them. Politics is inevitable under such circumstances. Because she did not recognize that and failed to take politics as a fact of work life, she was miserable and unprepared to deal with what was going on around her. Eventually she decided to accept the politics as a fact-of-life frame and asked me to help her learn the ropes. She was a good student and now has a very successful career. She never became a maneuverer, but she could defend herself with some impressive street fighting by the time we finished our work together.

GETTING PAST ASSUMPTIONS

Creative insights and frames are of little value if they are not communicated effectively to others. Many great ideas have fallen on deaf ears because their advocates didn't know how to connect them to the interests of others. People often become so enamored with what they consider a good idea that they fail to position it effectively. Skilled politicians, however, know that even great ideas need to be sold. They also know that assumptions often stand in the way of such sales. All of us slip easily into assumptions about other people and what they are likely to say. This is especially true when we know people well or when we categorize them quickly based on some surface quality. Skilled politicians achieve versatility in their thinking in part by recognizing one of the primary obstacles that block effective dealings with others—assumptions. They are skeptical of easy categorization and alert to the limitations of even the most astute judgments. They are careful not to squander their insights by casting them like pearls before swine to those too attracted to their own ideas to consider new ones or those whose preconceived assumptions will likely block their reception.

POLITICAL ADVANTAGE #5

The most effective politicians convey a strong interest in what other people are saying to them. They don't impose their views on others so much as manage their interactions so that others will feel they contributed considerably to the development of those views.

To ensure that insights and frames are given their best hearing, skilled politicians operate like detectives. They ask questions. They test the waters to see if others are likely to be receptive to their ideas. "What would you do at this juncture, Jeff?" or "Something you said earlier made me think of a possible solution. It's not quite formed yet but I'll try to explain it" are other ways of involving others in the creation of an idea that is already pretty well formulated.

Astute politicians know that most people resist new ideas, whether insightful or not, because they dislike uncertainty and/or taking risks. And so often they prefer the status quo, no matter how deficient, over change. For this reason, it is wise to involve those with veto power in the formulation of a solution that begins with your own insightful idea. I frequently meet highly competent people who've become frustrated or angry because their ideas haven't been given a fair hearing. They consider the people rejecting them idiots of the first order who wouldn't recognize a good idea if it hit them over the head. Usually the people rejecting these ideas are not idiots; often they're territorial or afraid of losing face if someone else's bright ideas are accepted over theirs. A good deal of political behavior is motivated by envy. There are times, of course, when an issue is so pressing and the need for a solution so demanding that taking time to include everyone in the final decision is not realistic. In most cases, however, even great ideas need to be conveyed with sensitivity to potential resistance.

As one junior executive in a recreation industry learned, "Rational arguments don't work when they infringe on egos." Competence alone, he explains, gets him just so far. Good ideas are only as good as they're salable. And he's right. As the senior VP of one of the world's largest insurance companies advises, "People need to feel you're working with them. That's smart politics. You draw the line if they're wrecking people's lives," he says, but in most cases, "you have to have the agility to work with people and to identify what matters to them when you're proposing ideas." So whether you like your boss or not, by learning to work with him or her you teach yourself to be flexible and you gain respect. Another successful computer executive offers a similar view: "In general, the situations I didn't handle well were because I lost my objectivity and patience. Those I do handle well are because I'm prepared to review options and can frame them with an appreciative balance of passion and objectivity." Here again value comes from learning to respond in ways not natural to you. And from a wise beyond-his-years manager comes an observation to remember: "Being right is interesting but it's often irrelevant." Often being flexible is admired more.

Given that there are almost always other people to convince before moving on an idea, it's usually wise to think in terms of an incremental and creative approach to solving problems. Consider the next case involving a dilemma faced by the manager of a computer products company, NAC. How would you solve this problem using an incremental approach?

THE RUDE MANAGER CASE

Your company, NAC, has worked with the APEX corporation for several years. You know the vice president of human resources rather well, and he always recommends NAC to his managers. However, you've learned that one of APEX's new managers, Charles, yells at people—his employees, and now yours as well. Susan, your star salesperson, says she doesn't want to work for Charles. She described a situation in which she was at APEX talking on the telephone. For some odd reason, Charles erroneously assumed that she was talking to a friend. He screamed, "Get off the phone!" Then he said angrily, while pointing his finger at her, "Don't ever let me catch you on a personal call again or you're out of here. Got it?" You recently learned that Charles is going through a tough divorce and often is very short-tempered. You'd like to have Susan continue working with APEX, but you don't want to lose her.

First, you should identify your primary goal and secondary goals, if you have them. Once you've gathered some insight on the situation, you can move on to framing. What frames will you use to describe the situation, as you see it, to Susan? Think creatively. How would you describe Charles and his current situation when talking with her? Will you approach him, or is there another way to proceed with a greater political upside? What options do you have? Should you involve the VP of human resources or even let him handle the situation? Go back to steps 1 through 8 to determine your goals and options.

Using the incremental approach, identify your ultimate goal, then list the smaller goals you can achieve more easily that may lead to achieving your ultimate one. Is your ultimate goal to change Charles's behavior or to convince Susan that she *can* deal with people like this and needs to learn how to benefit her career? Another option for an ultimate goal is to be able to retain the client and Susan, while keeping her at work for the client company. Or do you have another ultimate goal?

This kind of incremental thinking is difficult because most of us focus on ultimate goals. When we fail to reach them because they are too ambitious, many of us quit. In difficult, politically challenging situations, it's better to think in terms of incremental goals.

Now think in terms of incremental gains in achieving the ultimate goal. What smaller goals can you achieve early on? Which ones after those? All should be leading toward the achievement of the ultimate goal. Perhaps you identified some incremental goals with regard to Susan only, such as goal A: giving Susan a break by sending in another candidate to work with Charles for now. A1 might be convincing Susan that she is not part of the problem but part of the solution. A2 and A3 might be providing coaching for Susan on how to deal with rude people like Charles. Goal B then could be getting Susan to agree to give it another try with your support. Goals B1 through B4 could be levels of success in Susan's political skill development, with specific emphasis on ways to respond to Charles if he is rude again. Finally, goal C would be giving Susan the confidence and skills to deal with Charles's rudeness.

Incremental goals also could be established for the manager. The first goal (A) could be a conversation between you and Charles about Susan's concerns. A1 through A4 would be levels of improvement in the relationship. Goal B might involve meeting with the HR director, if need be, or convincing Charles to allow a coach to work with him, perhaps at your company's expense. If he isn't willing to do that or you feel that opportunity shouldn't be offered, then goal B might be his willingness to change his style when dealing with your employees, especially Susan. Incremental goals B1 through B4 would involve points of progress toward goal C: a good working relationship with Susan.

An approach that indirectly persuades might involve assigning Susan to work with Charles's boss as well as with him. This might cause Charles to consider the way he treats her without anyone having to intervene. Whether you inform his boss of your concerns or merely let things unfold depends on what you consider possible. Perhaps you can think of an insightful solution that involves a novel approach, such as convincing Susan that this is the perfect political test case for her and a critical part of her development. Let her know that, in a way, she's lucky to have come across Charles. This is framing. In this case, you reframe what Susan believes is a terrible state of affairs as an opportunity to learn how to manage bullies.

A SUMMARY THOUGHT FROM AN INSIGHTFUL MAN

Years ago I was fortunate enough to interview the late Douglas Edwards, the pioneering television journalist who anchored CBS evening news from its inception in 1948 until 1962. Shortly before retiring from broadcasting, he talked with me by phone. He said:

> You see things in congressional debates . . . and committee meetings sometimes that you think could have been handled much better had there been a little more tact, a little more patience. People have lost their temper, when they probably could have been [more] viable than they were if the question had been phrased in a more tactful way. I think a lot of persuasion has to do with tact—with the way something is worded. As the old saying goes, you get more with honey than with salt. I think it's true in interrogations and daily life. If you do it well you don't have to always be on pins and needles. Sometimes in daily intercourse there are ticklish matters that have to be rather carefully thought out before they're articulated. I try not to hurt anybody. Once in a while you have to be brutally blunt, but those times are very few and far between.

Douglas Edwards was successful not because he was slick but because he gave thought to his responses. He was a believer in considering the views of others. He respected people and seemed to possess a sincere desire to learn from them. During our interview, he asked me what I thought made my parents tune in to his TV program each night. I told him it was his ability to talk to millions of people as if he were speaking to each of them individually. "That's a compliment," he said, and told me that was something he learned at radio station WSB in Atlanta, where he got his journalism education:

> When I first started at WSB, a man named Lambdin Kay, a radio pioneer who'd started in the 1920s told me, "Remember, Doug, that although you're working on a 50,000-watt radio station that covers the Southeast—as the [Atlanta] *Journal* covers Dixie like the dew—when you talk into these microphones you're talking to groups of two people, maybe one—three at the most. Don't think of talking to a million or half a million people. Remember you're talking to one or two. Communicate with them. Talk to them. Talk personally to them." I think that was very good advice. Don't you? Because when you sit down in front of a TV camera as I do every day . . . and the audience is 8 or 12 million people . . . you'd go out of your mind if you decided you had to accommodate all of them, so I'd rather think I'm just talking to a few friends.

Edwards's method of talking to "a few good friends" when talking to millions may seem like common sense. But at that time, in the new business of television news, it was truly insightful because so few people were doing it. Insight isn't necessarily an earthshaking discovery; more often it is a slight change in perception that makes a world of difference. In any field, being open to new ways of doing things invites insight and—with a little luck—greater success.

CHAPTER FOUR

ADVANCE WORK AND
GETTING GOOD ON YOUR FEET

INTUITION AND INSIGHT can help you understand politically charged situations, but they mean very little unless you convert that understanding into strategies that work. Effective politicians examine a situation to determine whether they should use political strategies and tactics before an event (i.e., an important meeting), during the event—or both. They're experts at *advance work*; in other words, they know how to create conditions ahead of time that facilitate their ultimate goals, in the same way that Yankee Stadium's original designers drew the outfield to suit Babe Ruth's strengths as a hitter.[1]

Pat Bishop was an "advance work apprentice" when I became her coach. She had already recognized her need to plan more before speaking and had surpassed some of her colleagues as a result, but she wanted to learn more. As senior vice president for an executive placement company, she knew all about selling her products—skilled people—to outsiders. She also knew that selling inside was equally important. I rarely saw her jump into situations without considerable advance thinking. This is not to say that she took her sweet time. Like much of the advance thinking I'll discuss in this chapter, Pat's advance work didn't take long, yet it had beneficial long-term effects. "I try to put myself in the shoes of the party I am trying to persuade by asking myself 'What is going on for them besides my request?' In other words, what is the context in which my request is going to be viewed? What goals are they trying to achieve? What can I do to support those goals? I try to think of all these things before I begin to talk. I get the facts and prepare my arguments. It's not enough to be technically competent; you need to have the respect of the people you're dealing with and know well what they want."

Many politically naive people don't take time to consider which situational conditions will suit them best. They dive headfirst into situations, without thinking of ways to facilitate their success. The politically astute, however, never jump into a new situation without preparing. A great example is Mike, one of my former MBA marketing students, who now works for one of the largest computer technology companies in the world. "If you know your man well, you know his hot issues," Mike told me. He knows he works for a company that is focused on process issues. At meetings, questions always arise about how to get things done. He knows too that once a process has been described effectively to people above him, the next issue is who's going to do it. "I offer to take care of this and that. I get people to agree and pitch in." He learned early on that "one way to make yourself valuable is to save other people's time." This is how he explains his approach: "There's always a set of stakeholders my boss has to deal with. I assess what their needs will be, and I keep her out of the ins and outs of petty stuff or things I can handle just as easily. I don't go taking bullets. I just arrange to get things done without taking any more of her time than absolutely necessary. Fortunately, my company encourages taking risks, especially in the service of looking after your manager."

Not all companies are process-oriented, nor do all encourage protecting the boss from trivial demands. "Where I work everyone's keen on new ideas," Bill Collins said of his advanced flight technology company. "You can't just blurt them out. You have to feel out who's in charge or has influence and assess the current status of things. You can't make the mistake of trying to fix something they don't see as broken. First, establish the problem or try to find someone of influence that understands there is a problem and try your solution out on him before going public." As he told me, Collins learned this the hard way:

> I tried introducing a new data collection system in our Assembly and Test department early on in my career here. One of the senior managers from another division jumped all over me about details. I thought the presentation was going to be a flop. Fortunately, a senior vice president put him in his place, and my credibility was instantly raised. But the whole scene could have been avoided had I sought out senior management support for the idea prior to presenting. I could have been coached on delivery and on what to expect from my audience. Now I review anything I think might be controversial with peers or senior management before going public. In an organization of mostly engineers, you have to collect all the data before drawing conclusions. So, my rule is—When asked for an opinion, first try out some of the supporting facts before presenting the conclusion. It's just good business sense.

Collins is the CEO of his division now, so clearly he has benefited from thought in advance of action. He isn't timid. He calculates risks, considers options, and weighs benefits and potential losses. This separates him from political novices. And if you were to meet him, you'd see that he is not a smooth-talking executive who's out of touch with his people. He may be wearing a crisp shirt and tie, but he's always talking with one person on the assembly line or another in the offices, learning how they think. That's advance work.

No matter what level you're at in an organization, advance work is critical. Before you take risks, stand up for what you believe in, try to make a change in the system, settle scores, or correct misperceptions, you must learn who stands to gain and who stands to lose if you get your way, as well as how these people think and what matters to them. If you do not, then any success you may be lucky enough to have is going to be short-lived. Those who rush to fix what they see as problems in organizations rarely get what they're after. As the rest of this chapter demonstrates, there are a number of skills under the umbrella of advance work, and you need all of them.

THINKING ON YOUR FEET

Advance work is only half the battle when presenting ideas in politically adept ways. Thinking well on your feet is critical. What do you do when you have a great idea but getting anyone interested seems a Sisyphean task, especially when there are people pushing down on the boulder, making the climb even more difficult? Do you keep pushing? "Not me," says Ellen Nichols, a senior manager at a Hartford-based insurance company. "You have to sense when you're in a totally inflexible situation and the other party has no room to move (and you know going to your boss . . . won't work). That's when you give in graciously. You have to know when to fold the cards. And you have to know to say something like 'I know this isn't what I really need for my department, but I understand that it's what the company needs to do now.' " Nichols adds that you should never have to force someone to do something they really shouldn't do, nor should you behave like a bad child. "You have to know when to stop fighting for something. I'm always able to walk away feeling okay if I can say, 'I may not agree with that decision, but I understand why it was made.' "

Nichols believes in starting over the next day—starting every day in fact—fresh. "I detach myself from decisions that don't go my way. They're business decisions. I let them go. If you can do this, then you remain open and honest with people. Just start over fresh and move on."

In so many coaching situations, people ask me, "How should I tell him this?" or "What should I do to make her do this?" These questions demonstrate a lack of an on-your-feet repertoire of responses. You can't assume that everything will go a certain way once you begin talking. That's just not the way human interactions play out—neither at work nor in life. Whenever Bill Collins, the flight technology CEO, faces a situation where he knows he'll have difficulty in convincing people, he considers how he might let them convince themselves. He worries less about what he'll tell others than he does about how he'll encourage them to consider the same challenges he's been dealing with long before the meeting. Once people know the problem you're facing, Collins has discovered, the more willing they'll be to help you fix it.

Thinking on your feet is about keeping yourself from slipping into easy answers and old habits when a fresh approach might work better. If you can't think on your feet, then your days will likely mirror Reginald Strongbrow's.

Reginald is a fictitious character based on many real people I've coached, met, taught, and worked with—a technically competent person without a political bone in his body. He is incapable of recognizing, let alone managing, much of what happens to him in the course of a day. You can see from this description of one of his mornings how he contributes to his own political plight.

Reginald arrives at his office at 8:20 A.M., ten minutes before most of his coworkers arrive, to try to get a good start on the day. As he hangs up his jacket, his boss, Michael Simmons (vice president of operations), stops in the doorway.

"Strongbrow, you look tired today," he says, more as an observation than as an expression of concern. "Family problems?"

"No, I'm fine," Reginald says.

"Okay," Michael says as he moves on. "Get some rest."

Reginald sits at his desk, wondering whether he really looks tired and what Michael meant by that comment about his family. When he glances up at the clock, it's already 9 A.M. He attempts to put the remark behind him, like so many similar ones he's puzzled over in the past, and starts to peruse the mail on his desk. He comes across a copy of the divisional newsletter. The front page includes a photo and story about his project team. Reginald does not appear in the photo, nor is he mentioned in the story. He takes the newsletter down the hall to the office of John Smith, project coordinator.

"If you have a moment," Reginald said, "I just saw the story in the newsletter."

As Smith rises from his desk and joins Reginald to look at the newsletter, he quickly replies: "Oh, that was a spur-of-the-moment thing. The editor wanted a team photo, but I think you were away that morning. We had to meet a print deadline. No big deal, though, Reg—right?" Smith slaps Reginald on the back.

This isn't the first time Reginald has been overlooked, but he decides not to belabor the issue. "It was a spontaneous thing, then?"

"Yeah. It isn't even a good photo, and the story is lousy. You're lucky you got out of it."

As Reginald returns to his office, he gets a call from the division secretary. "You have a meeting with Frank Pillar in ten minutes." The secretary explains that Pillar, the company's CEO, wants an update on the project. Reginald isn't sure why Pillar wants him to present the information, given that Smith has always done so previously.

Reginald arrives at the conference room early to prepare his thoughts. Pillar enters with Reginald's boss at his side.

"Hey there, Reginald," Pillar says, smiling. "Michael, check out Reginald's new suit—and what a tie! We must be paying him too much."

Reginald forces a smile in return. He can take a joke, but he wonders what Pillar means. They certainly aren't paying him what he deserves. He considers himself to have good taste, but he never wears anything too stylish. The suit isn't even new. Reginald lets the comment pass, thinking "It was probably harmless—no derogatory meaning or message." Perhaps he is overtired.

The meeting begins. Reginald starts to explain why team progress on the project has been delayed. Pillar and Simmons glance at each other, then Simmons interrupts.

"You're telling us that after all the money we poured into this project, the competition is going to leave us standing at the starting gate?"

Reginald bolts upright. "I didn't say that. I was about to say—"

"This is certainly a surprise to me," Simmons says, looking over at Pillar, who is fixated on Reginald.

"I don't like surprises, Reg," Pillar says coldly.

"If I could just explain. . . ."

"I don't need explanations. I need action. Fix it."

Some discussion between Simmons and Pillar follows, but Reginald hears only parts of it. He is too busy dealing with his own annoyance and frustration.

The rest of the day is relatively uneventful. None of the project team members stops by to ask about the meeting with Pillar. Reginald tries to work but is plagued with thoughts about Simmons's comments regarding his appearance and his family, about being excluded from the team photo and then being drawn into an unexpected debacle with Pillar and Simmons. He turns to his computer; perhaps he should e-mail Pillar and copy Simmons, explaining the good points he'd been unable to make because of their interruptions. Yes, the delay was problematic, but it had been unavoidable due to holdups and mistakes in another division. But then he thinks better of it. Pointing fingers has never been his style.

At 6 P.M., as Reginald prepares to leave for the day, Michael Simmons appears in the doorway, saying, "You don't have to worry about the Japan trip. John Smith will be going."

Reginald's jaw drops. He'd been planning that trip for months. It's an important one for the company. "What do you mean?"

"Well, after today you don't expect Frank to feel comfortable sending you, do you? Look at it this way—at least you still have a job."

As Reginald walks to his car, he feels drained. Japan was going to be his chance to achieve some vital visibility. Now he needs to lay low for a few months before even hoping to regain Pillar's trust and regard. He thinks of John Smith going to Japan in his stead. No doubt he'd be celebrating tonight, while Reginald tries to find solace in a book. The possibility that John has undermined him creeps into Reginald's mind. Before it can establish a foothold, he pushes it away.

"It's nobody's fault but mine," he says aloud, as he turns the key in the ignition, then backs out of the parking space that he realizes might soon have another name on it.

Reginald Strongbrow probably arrived where he is today thanks to hard work and loyalty. Both are admirable qualities and both are necessary for advancement. Without political know-how, however, Reginald has gotten about as far as he will go in a company that promotes the likes of Smith, Simmons, and Pillar. Reginald functions one step behind his detractors. Clearly he lacks political intuition or ignores what intuition he does have. He isn't politically insightful either; he seems to jump into the events of the day without advance work. Even a few minutes of reflection before taking an action would help Reginald considerably.

Reginald is not good on his feet. He is a political purist; he does not think in terms of political strategy at work. This would be fine if he worked with other people like himself in a minimally or moderately political arena. Instead, he appears to be working with street fighters and maneuverers in a highly or pathologically political environment. In short, Reginald is in over his head.

When confronted with a comment like "You're looking tired today," the purist will likely think: "It was considerate of him to take an interest." By contrast, political street fighters will immediately consider whether this person is attempting to advance some agenda. The more controlling (and paranoid) maneuverers think:

I'd better watch my back. Simmons may have had no ulterior motive when he commented about Reginald's apparent fatigue. The second remark about "family problems," though, should have put Reginald on guard, but he let it pass. By not responding, he allowed a detrimental perception to take on life, possibly to become grist for the rumor mill and a part of his image. He might have replied, "Haven't had my coffee yet," or "I've been burning the midnight oil again on the Kemper project," or, smiling, "None of us look great at this hour." He could have responded to the comment about his family with a straightforward denial or a humorous retort, such as "From the way people look around here in the morning, there must be a lot of family problems." Whatever his choice of response, Reginald has a political responsibility to himself. He is at least 75 percent responsible for the way people treat him. We all are. Meanings are tossed around all day everyday, and it's up to each of us to manage them.

All day long Reginald had chances to do so, and all day long he failed. Reginald should not have allowed himself to be the team spokesperson and the bearer of bad news, especially since fellow team member John Smith had previously delivered all the good news. If Reginald truly believed that his team needed him to step up, he should have at least insisted that they come along to support him. Better still, he could have kicked the job back to John Smith or insisted the meeting be postponed until everyone could be present. Reginald didn't demonstrate any leadership potential by going alone to the meeting; he just put himself in harm's way. And he did it again when he failed to convey the reason his team had been delayed and when he allowed Simmons to give the Japan trip to Smith without so much as a protest. Reginald may be a bright person, but his political knowledge and skill is sorely lacking. If he doesn't change his style, he'll soon be company road kill.

Yet there are people like Reginald everywhere. You, a colleague, or someone you mentor may be one of them. Much of what happened to Reginald could have been managed ahead of time by the use of advance political strategies, which involve arranging conditions or managing perceptions that will favor a preferred agenda. Such actions include:

- Getting to know people who can be helpful in certain regards
- Meeting with these people before taking an important action
- Floating trial balloons (testing out an idea by mentioning it or a portion of it to see how people respond)
- Performing impression management to advance an agenda
- Anticipating and preparing to deal with obstacles

These are all forms of advance work that can help you manage perceptions—and your career. Being cooperative (or uncooperative) when people expect otherwise can guide or influence the course of events. Reginald was far too cooperative, and his peers and bosses took advantage of that. If he had veered from this behavior, he might have gotten the upper hand. Unfortunately, Reginald wasn't thinking on his feet.

Political strategies used to respond to challenges, personal attacks, and assaults on an agenda are examples of *on-your-feet politics*. Dealing with conflict, deflecting anger and revising the direction of an interaction are other methods. Where the stakes are high, circumstances often call for both advance work and on-your-feet politics—by first setting the stage and then responding effectively to resistance or challenge.

How might Reginald have acted on his feet? Instead of letting Smith off far too easily with regard to the newsletter, he should have at least said, "John, I'm not taking this issue as lightly as you are," or "Just assure me that it won't happen again and I'll be on my way." When he found out that he was expected at a meeting in only forty-five minutes, he should have sought John out and insisted he come along, or even postponed the meeting. If neither of those options was available, he could have rounded up some other team members and advised them to attend and field questions relevant to their specialties. At the very least, he could have gone to the meeting and informed the two executives that John had the information they needed but was unavailable until later that day.

When dealing with senior people in such circumstances, it's important to show them you are not an easy target or scapegoat. If they act as if they hold all the cards, let them know that you have a few yourself (if you do) and are freely choosing to cooperate. Here's an example of how I dealt with such a situation. Although I enjoyed a generally positive relationship with a senior colleague (let's call him Wilson) who supervised a program I was working on, he immediately rejected an idea I'd proposed for a new executive training program. "Can't be done," Wilson said dismissively. I tried to provide him with evidence of the idea's viability. "No. Absolutely not," he interrupted, and turned away from me to write something on the whiteboard. I was taken aback. I thought perhaps I'd failed to provide an adequate explanation. Again, I started to speak. "You're wasting your breath," he said, still writing. Then he turned and looked down at me (at least that's how it felt given his status advantage) and said, "It's nonnegotiable. That's all there is to it."

This is an excellent example of a choice point. Wilson was my senior by years and rank, a fact of which he was keenly aware. The emphatic nature of his comments was, it seemed, intended to shut down all further discussion. The intensity of his expression reinforced this intention. He'd insisted on bringing our interaction to a halt. This called for a defensive response. But given his mood, I knew that responding in kind (in other words, aggressively) surely would have made things worse.

I began to walk away from him to give myself a chance to think and him the impression that he'd won. Then I turned back. "Okay," I said. "You win. I just need one thing." His look warned me "This better be good," but also seemed to imply there was room for progress. I asked for something he could easily approve, a mere pilot version of my original proposal, which included out-of-class negotiation experiences for the executives I was training. I suggested that the executives could record their findings in a journal, and later, a few could be role-played in a short session. That way much of the work would be done outside the classroom, and the experiences could be linked to the other subjects my students were studying. Having given him some breathing room, I could practically see him ticking a checklist in his mind: that we had a good working relationship; that in the past, I'd helped him and he'd helped me. He shook his head, and I could almost detect a smile. "Fine," he replied, again turning back to the whiteboard.

This is an example of how advance work and on-your-feet political repertoires can work together. In this case, political advance work included developing a history of helping Wilson. Before, Wilson had the power to make or break careers at the drop of a word to the right people. We had developed a good relationship. Had I directly challenged his authority, it might have harmed our relationship, or, worse, I might have committed career suicide. I knew him well enough to believe that nudging him for a more reasonable response might work. It seemed preferable to putting my head down and retreating from the room, and in fact I would have lost at least some of his respect had I done so. To Wilson, abject surrender was worse than conflict. Because I was asking for only a portion of what I wanted, he wasn't forced to acquiesce in any large sense to a junior person. Based on our prior relationship and our "favor bank" balances, it was the least he could do. In this case, it was my advance work that allowed an on-my-feet request to succeed.

Positioning and defending our ideas and ourselves is a major part of what all of us do at work. Developing advance and on-your-feet repertoires of political strategies and tactics (both offensive and defensive) is critical to success. Yet most of us rely on what psychologists call "mental models"—what I've described as scripts—to respond to difficult situations. These scripts are often inadequate because too little advance work has gone into them. As a result, many of us slip unwittingly into modes of action that simply don't cut it.

Harvard business professor Chris Argyris explains that this kind of slipping into old habits keeps us from learning. We often delude ourselves when it comes to our actions—we assume they always match our principles and personal rules. In actuality, Argyris argues, most of what we do in reaction to stress isn't at all related to what we, when given time to think, would expect of ourselves: "Each of us has what I call an *espoused theory of action* based on principles and precepts that fit our intellectual backgrounds and commitments. But most of us have quite a different *theory-in-use* to which we resort in moments of stress. And very few of us are aware of the contradiction between the two. In short, most of us are consistently inconsistent in the way we act."[2]

Argyris explains that when faced with stress, we act in ways that avoid vulnerability, risk, embarrassment, and the appearance of incompetence. These defensive actions are a recipe for ineffective learning, or "antilearning"—slipping into habits of interpreting events that limit the ability to learn. For advance work and on-your-feet strategies to work effectively, they should be coordinated. Skilled politicians are very aware of the potential for disconnects between espoused theories of action and theories-in-use. They don't allow slips of this sort to happen. They do high-level advance work that involves consciously selecting courses of action that fit their philosophies and/or the culture of the company, and, as a result, learn to act in a way that increases the likelihood of their desired outcomes.

DOING THE ADVANCE WORK

Now that you understand how advance work and on-your-feet politics contribute to political success at work, let's take a closer look at how people have used both techniques to advance their careers. We'll start with advance work.

A Los Angeles–based senior executive recruiter told me that she looks for people who can "read the tea leaves." "It's difficult to describe," she explained, "but this involves an ability to foresee events that might hinder your progress or that of an important project." Proactive politicians recognize signs of impending career and project obstacles in time to deal with them. "My quest for power used to be so important," a California banking executive told me. "Over time I realized that more got done when I took an inquisitive, rather than bulldog, approach." She listened and learned how things were said and observed how they got done. "One day at a meeting when some people were refusing to make what they saw as a risky change in policy, I used this knowledge. I said in words they'd appreciate, 'Instead of embracing change, perhaps we should be embracing progress.' They liked that. Progress was important to them, change was threatening. Senior managers at that meeting never forgot I'd said that, and it made a big difference in my career."

Carly Fiorina used her knowledge of Hewlett-Packard's corporate culture when battling Walter Hewlett, son of H-P cofounder William Hewlett. The younger Hewlett was a formidable foe who opposed H-P's $25 billion merger with Compaq Computer. He had the clout of his name, huge financial support, and considerable shareholder sentiment on his side. Undaunted, Carly Fiorina did what seemed impossible. Using nostalgic photos of the company's risk-taking founders, she linked her own leadership with audacity. "This company has always been about being daring," she said in her speeches. In March of 2002, a few days before a crucial shareholders meeting, Fiorina sat down for dinner with all of H-P's directors except Hewlett. She asked them each to consider all the ramifications for the company if the merger failed. Next, she did something quite unexpected. Rather than stay around to cajole their support, she left the room. For more than an hour, the directors were able to speak candidly among themselves. When they asked her to return, Fiorina did so to overwhelming support. Within a few months Hewlett was gone and Fiorina was leading the merger.[3]

Carly Fiorina developed alliances under what seemed to be extremely adverse conditions. She expertly applied offensive politics: She knew whom she was dealing with; she demonstrated strong evidence in support of the merger and conviction in her beliefs. She refused to become involved in a shouting match; and she expertly lined up her ducks (obtained the support of key people). It was a masterful move.

Unfortunately, the merger came back to haunt Fiorina. When, in 2003, investors began to shift their focus from the excitement of the Compaq deal to the success of H-P's competitors IBM and Dell, Fiorina was criticized for failing to quickly strengthen H-P's position. Rather than building a strong offensive attack, she went on the defensive, firing three top sales executives after a massive shortfall in profits in the third quarter of 2004. But the downhill spiral continued. Not satisfied that she was heeding their warnings, board members began meeting without her. The alliances that allowed her to win the Compaq merger debate were not developed in time or sufficiently enough to save her from dismissal. Because she failed to do *after* the merger what she'd so expertly done *before* it, the CEO was asked to step down in February 2005.[4]

Perhaps the H-P profit losses were too great to overcome with political sophistication. But her precipitous fall suggests that Fiorina was not endeavoring to rally support in turning the company around and in presenting to the public a sense that she was not alone. Once the board began to see her as the enemy, there was no turning back.

Rallying support in difficult times is as necessary for senior people as it is for junior ones. As leadership expert Warren Bennis explains: "When leaders fail to form alliances, their legitimacy is questioned. Even when their cause is just, they may be perceived as rogues. And however they are perceived, their work is made harder by the absence of allies willing to share the burden of the enterprise, including its costs. Because leaders are, by definition, men and women who seem to stand apart, we tend to forget just how important coalition building is in the essential repertoire of leadership. In free societies, all leadership is the consequence of consensus and coalition building; it is never unilateral."[5]

No one is immune from the need for support. Some CEOs may come to believe they are, but they rarely last long. As Bennis argues, the Lone Ranger is dead — if he ever existed at all. "The perfect idea" is a myth. Neither people nor ideas stand the test of time completely on their own. They must be championed and supported, and most often that support is established long before an important decision.

Forming alliances is only one form of advance work. Others include:

- Establishing a sound track record
- Managing others' impressions of you
- Dismantling obstacles before decisions are made
- Framing ideas in appealing ways before promoting them

These behaviors set the stage for progress and therefore are imperative in situations where resistance is likely; they are also helpful when dealing with someone whose intentions are suspect or who has a poor reputation, or when you have reason to believe a past incident may interfere with progress.

"Giving them enough rope to hang themselves" is one example of a useful advance strategy for dealing with problematic people, especially those with a tendency to become arrogant. People who flaunt what they consider to be their strong suit will, in all likelihood, eventually do so with the wrong person. People who burn bridges risk angering someone who may someday have the power to make or break their careers. During a session on politics, a banking senior manager asked me how to deal with people who use politics as a vicious game. I told him that in my experience, that type of person almost always self-destructs. Granted, sometimes it's a long wait; but more often than not, these people will sink their own ships—and no one will be eager to save them.

THINKING AND ACTING ON YOUR FEET

Operating on your feet at work means being able to employ offensive and defensive tactics. A few examples of on-your-feet political acumen include:

- Having a sense of whether to confront a situation head-on or let time heal wounds

- Knowing whether to call in heavy artillery in the form of powerful supporters
- Asking a politically sensitive friend how to make amends with someone you've offended
- Recognizing when to apologize
- Providing an excuse that's acceptable in your company's culture if your behavior is questioned

Reginald Strongbrow was poor at a number of these and other forms of political on-your-feet tactics. For example, he didn't confront a number of situations head-on but rather allowed himself to slip into no-win situations, such as representing an absent team at a meeting and allowing the Japan trip to be taken away from him without murmuring a challenge. He knew nothing of garnering support or providing reasonable excuses for not doing things that might threaten his career. He didn't know how to handle situations in ways that would allow him to save face while not threatening the face of his superiors.

The editor of an in-house magazine for an East Coast–based paper products company told me of a time when he did what Reginald couldn't:

> I'll never forget when one of our best issues had just been printed and distributed. That day a senior VP telephoned me. He started yelling and screaming about how we'd misrepresented his division. He said the numbers in one of the articles were all wrong and carried on about our ineptitude, threatening never to let any of us into his area again. He was just plain wrong. We'd checked the figures twice with his assistant. He hung up the phone before I had a chance to tell him that. I was steaming when I walked into my boss's office. I told her the story. She listened, paused, and said, "Send him a rose." "A what?!" I said. I had a list of other, less appealing things on my mind to send him. But she repeated herself.

"Send him a rose. Not a real rose—send him a memo telling him how much we value working with him. Explain our policy of checking all numbers and let him know we did that in this case, but don't dwell on it. Then explain that we will issue a correction in the next edition of the magazine. Let him know that the most important thing to us is continuing what has been a very positive relationship." I had my reservations, to be sure. But I did as she suggested. Some weeks later I saw this guy in the hall. He walked up to me, shook my hand, and said, "I like working with you." That was all he said. It was enough. Apparently he likes roses.

CONSTRUCTIVE VS. DESTRUCTIVE APPROACHES

Both advance work and on-your-feet strategies can be of two forms: constructive and destructive. Constructive politicians do not attempt to dupe or backstab their opponents, nor do they use traps or spies. The political strategies are largely up front. In terms of advance work, constructive politics include such things as:

- Creating a positive impression—assuring that key people find you interesting and approachable
- Positioning—being in the right place at the right time
- Cultivating mentors—locating experienced advisors
- Lining up the ducks—making strategic visits to strategic peers, senior people, and support staff at which you mention your accomplishments and let them know what you can do for them
- Developing your favor bank—favors usually require reciprocation; by agreeing to—or even offering—favors, you make "deposits" in anticipation that someday, when you need to call in a chit, you will have the "currency" to do so

Destructive politics include:

- Poisoning the well—fabricating negative information about others, dropping defaming information into conversation and meetings in the hope of ruining the target's career chances
- Faking left while going right—leading others to believe you will take one action in order to increase the likelihood of succeeding via an entirely different maneuver; allowing or encouraging someone to think one condition exists when in reality another condition holds
- Deception—lying, for whatever reason
- Entrapment—steering or manipulating someone into a political position or action that results in embarrassment, failure, discipline, or job loss

Destructive political tactics are at best indirect and at worst downright malicious. During one of my consulting experiences I witnessed an executive, whom I'll call Ray, who was making the life of a junior colleague (I'll call her Eva) a living hell. Ray felt personally offended if anyone disagreed with him at meetings, but he got especially upset at Eva. Ray began insulting her at meetings, and eventually he sent memos to other senior executives detailing every instance where she'd made what he considered to be an error in judgment. His venomous approach started disturbing all those involved. It became clear he wanted her fired. My unenviable task was to help him understand that his hatred of Eva was casting him as unprofessional and petty in the eyes of his colleagues. In response, he began sending me derogatory e-mails questioning my credibility and raving about his own superiority. He made the mistake of not thinking about these e-mails before sending them. Eventually his e-mails became his own undoing. I read aloud excerpts from a sample of his e-mails—letting him hear his own ravings. I explained how negatively similar e-mails he'd sent to Eva had been interpreted by the very people who may once have been on his side. Ultimately he gave up sending e-mails and went back to doing his job—one he wouldn't have held for much longer without the positive intervention of people who had tired of his pettiness. Destructive politicians who go too far often destroy their own careers.

CONSTRUCTIVE ADVANCE WORK

What would you do if you believed that a manager in another division of your company would try to destroy an important team project, were he to learn of it? Would you keep him in the dark or attempt to bring him into the loop and deal with his objections directly? This was the quandary faced by a computer products senior manager; he decided to take the secretive route. When his team's project proposal was ready, he arranged to meet with a senior vice president. At the meeting, he learned that the manager he'd attempted to keep in the dark had heard about the proposal via the grapevine—and would be attending the meeting by conference call.

Constructive advance work would have prevented this outcome. In most organizations, it's best to expect that a secret won't remain a secret for long. In this case, the manager could have informed the other manager of the team meetings early on. He might have said, "We don't have anything definitive yet, but I wanted you to know that we're exploring options." After that, he could delay further progress reports if that seemed wise, making an FYI phone call just before the meeting with the senior VP. This type of advance work usually makes fewer enemies than outright secretiveness. Granted, its effectiveness depends on skillful political management of a perceived detractor. Informing the other manager of a proposal in the works could have invited resistance, even a recommendation to senior management to kill it. But the political fallout of leaving a powerful enemy completely in the dark posed a much more serious threat to both the project and the career of the senior manager who did so. There are other ways to circumvent potential obstacles by adversaries. One is to get to senior management first. Build a case for the project, and suggest that some objections might be forthcoming. This approach is called "inoculation"—in other words, informing people ahead of time that they might hear negative things about an idea, project, or person and giving them good reasons to ignore or reject such attacks, should they occur. Some professional politicians have been known to do this when they expected that voters would learn of a skeleton in their closet. They'd tell the voters themselves before the leak occurred and offer an explanation or excuse for the actions in question. Should a detractor then attempt to bring up the politician's controversial actions, voters will not be surprised or shocked since the issue had been addressed and justifications provided.

In business, constructive advance work involves managing expected difficulties—smoothing the path by making allies out of potential enemies or disarming them altogether. Intuition will help you identify the likely actions of such aggressors and develop insightful strategies to deal with them. One successful manager referred to "the sniff test" when describing her constructive advance work. "If something doesn't smell good, it probably isn't," she said. Even if the situation passes the sniff test, this manager doesn't rush in. "Having the right plan is vital, but so is having the right people supporting it. I'm not talking about the kind of person who can't do anything because they're always taking a careful, ready, aim, aim, aim approach. Once you've done the work up front and gotten the right support, you're ready to do something."

Had Reginald Strongbrow been more politically astute, he would have already determined which of his peers weren't looking out for his best interests and would have been cultivating those likely to be on his side; he would have developed allies who in turn would have insisted that he be included in the project team photo shoot, and Bill Simmons would have been far less likely to put him "on the carpet" by asking him to represent the team alone—and that's just for starters.

You needn't be high up on the corporate ladder to get to know the right people—and you need not be climbing it at all to use advance work to make things happen. Every time someone checks out a library book in Louisiana they can thank Sallie Farrell, whose political intuition and diligent attention to advance work made it all happen. In 1954 she and her supporters received $2 million from the state legislature to build a new state library building. Farrell led a campaign to obtain the money and to establish models for libraries throughout the United States. She is widely credited as being a core factor in the establishment of a statewide network of libraries.

Cheerful, poised, and a determined charmer (according to the local *Sunday Advocate*), this southern librarian surprised many with the number of people she knew in state government. "I had a little file of all the legislators with a thumbnail sketch of each one, with things to identify them like 'gold tooth' or 'red hair,'" she said. Early on, she traveled the state convincing citizens and community leaders that they needed a library. She and colleagues Katherine Adams and Sarah Jones set up a demonstration program where small-scale libraries were constructed in local parishes, which enabled people to see what they were missing. Skeptics were converted at no initial cost to them. The librarians created files of letters from interested citizens as evidence to support their initiative. This is true offensive yet constructive politics—giving people a taste of what they'll receive if they follow your lead. It is also the antithesis of the stereotypes that give politics a bad name.

Another example of the power of advance work is Richard Parson's climb to the top of AOL-Time Warner. Business experts were taken by surprise when Parsons surpassed purported AOL-Time Warner heir apparent Robert Pittman in the race for the top spot. Chief executive Gerald Levin seemed at one time to favor Pittman; what happened? People were not paying attention to Parson's advance work—how he spoke to and acted toward others long before the CEO spot opened. Times had changed since Levin engineered the merger of AOL and Time Warner. A new leader would need to have new ideas, exude confidence, inspire people, and be capable of building consensus. Parsons was seen as this kind of people person. "Dick is big and physically imposing, making him a scary cuss," one senior executive said of the new CEO. "But he has an unbelievable code of honor that people trust. He can kick you from one end of the room to another, but he's fair, he doesn't leave you bloody and in the end, you still love him." Parsons earned a reputation as a peace-maker while president of Time Warner, where he'd also served on the board for many years. He calmed warring factions and earned admiration for the way he ran the company when Levin stepped away in 1997 to grieve after the death of his son. Parsons proved himself a diplomat during the AOL-Time Warner merger. He was seen as a serious businessman who never took himself too seriously. He engaged in the kinds of advance politics that moved him to the front of an extremely talented, hardworking pack of contenders.[6]

Advance work was a large part of the reason why FBI chief Louis J. Freeh was able to survive what the *Washington Post* termed "massive problems with the FBI crime lab and the mishandling of the Atlanta Olympic bombing case [and] . . . its handling of the investigation into whether former Los Alamos Nuclear Laboratory scientist Wen Ho Lee mishandled nuclear secrets." Nonetheless, the *Post* said, "Freeh, who proved to be an adroit political operative, withstood the attacks that followed each episode, maintaining strong ties to the key lawmakers who oversee his agency."[7] When first nominated to run the FBI by President Bill Clinton in 1993, Freeh was viewed as largely apolitical. Yet he established strong alliances with members of both parties and became one of Washington's wiliest politicians. Was this due to an overnight transformation? The better explanation is Freeh's keen sense of timing, a crucial component of offensive politics. He challenged Attorney General Janet Reno when she refused to appoint an independent counsel to investigate Democratic campaign fund-raising practices, which gained him credibility on the Republican side of the aisle. He survived cover-up allegations after the 1993 siege of Waco, Texas, and he misstepped and, many say, botched major spy cases, yet his popularity on Capitol Hill kept him afloat. Why? Freeh knew how to make friends. Juliette Kayyem of Harvard's Kennedy School of Government described Freeh as "charming." "He brings you in," she said. "He gave us a sense of what was going on in the millennium [bombing] investigation, and he followed up with personalized thank-you letters. . . . It made you feel good about the

FBI in a 'Gosh, he seems like a nice guy' way. At the same time, he might be asking for the world."[8]

Freeh remained at the FBI's helm until May 2001 and was under no pressure to resign when he decided to leave the post. According to former Senate Judiciary Committee investigator Kris Kolesnik, Freeh used information as currency and was quick to pick up the phone "to do his mea culpas" when a scandal broke. "He confesses his sins before the high priests in Congress, but they don't give him penance; they give him more agents and money."[9] Certainly Freeh was not without his successes, including extensive improvements in the FBI. But even these successes might not have saved the job of a less politically astute director. Freeh appreciated the concerns of his constituency and didn't fail to let them know it. The politician who lays the groundwork to support him- or herself in rough times accumulates what psychologists call "idiosyncrasy credits."[10] These are goodwill credits that you can spend when you're in trouble, causing problems that might otherwise terminate most careers simply to disappear.

STAY CONSTRUCTIVE ON YOUR FEET

Although Reginald Strongbrow's reactions were too timid and ill-prepared, many people's are too aggressive. Adept politicians remind themselves that *when someone attacks their idea, that person is not attacking them personally.* This is a very important distinction, because people have a tendency to retaliate when they feel threatened. The smart politician refuses to interpret criticism as a personal attack and instead understands it's directed toward the subject at hand. Understandably, doing this requires a good amount of self-management. When someone threatens our goals, it's much easier to take the attack personally and lash out in response. Doing so rarely leads to positive outcomes.

One of my favorite examples of good political footwork comes from an interview I did with a proficient negotiator whose career depends on making high-stakes, high-profile deals. He rarely finds himself cornered, but when a co-negotiator begins to press an advantage too hard or attempts to overwhelm by force, the negotiator responds with a nonverbal defensive strategy. "I look right at him. Not into his eyes. That's important. I look directly at the bridge of the nose between his eyes and leave my focus there while he's talking. It looks to him as if I'm staring sternly, but since I'm not looking into his eyes, he doesn't turn away. It's unsettling, so most people move away from their position."

This nonverbal, on-your-feet move may be used constructively or destructively. This negotiator employed it to unsettle someone who was trying to box him into a corner—a very constructive move. There are many other nonverbal defensive moves, including pacing, delay tactics; and expressing anger, disappointment, puzzlement, disinterest, or annoyance. Ordinarily, you should use defensive tactics to buy time or shift someone's perception without insulting, trapping, or otherwise harming the person.

Acting on your feet means constructively redefining situations (e.g., suggesting that a heated discussion is a "debate" rather than a "fight") and redirecting the course of an interaction (e.g., responding to criticism as if it were constructive advice).

CREDIT YOUR DETRACTOR

Crediting your detractor is a very important technique for avoiding interpersonal warfare. Usually you can use some element of a detractor's statement to advance your agenda. Recognizing this element requires careful listening and an ability to shrug off the potential insult in what has been said. Politicians often give away credit to avoid an impasse. Here are some of the kinds of statements they make:

"I hadn't thought of that."
"Interesting."
"That's exactly the kind of thinking we need to get this off the ground."
"What Michael said earlier was perfect."

"If we try to put these three ideas together, we could come up
*   with something amazing."*
"Where have you been all my life?"
"That idea is terrific, and if we implement what you suggested
*   early on and follow up with my idea, I think we'll have a*
*   winner."*

These kinds of credit-granting statements can keep an idea alive
when it's under attack. Most good ideas are a combination of concepts anyway, so when you expect disparagers to trash your ideas,
look for ways to connect theirs to yours.

Here's how one manager used this approach.

Recently a highly respected original partner in our company visited one of our remote locations. In her brief visit
she decided that the office was "dead." She told the chairman that there was little activity, little synergy in efforts. He
reacted immediately by storming into my office. He insisted
that I visit the office myself in the upcoming week. My initial reaction was to defend and let him know that half the
staff was in training. I wanted to telephone the partner to say
the same things. Instead, I decided to take the high road, to
treat her as I would want to be treated. I called her and listened to her. I told the chairman that I'd talked with her and
that all of her impressions would be examined. I'd essentially decided that this partner was too important a player
and that the best outcome would be to give her the impression that I was open to feedback and credited her observations. The partner and chairman were very positive in their
reactions. She said some very complimentary things about
the division. I learned later that for a number of reasons her
real agenda was to feel like she was still part of the team. So
it wouldn't have done any good to fight with her about how
"dead" the division was, because that wasn't the real issue.

GIVE THEM A CHANCE TO DO THE RIGHT THING

This is a very useful on-your-feet political strategy that involves redefining an issue or action. People often offend each other; it's human nature. There is a definite difference, however, between accidental offense and intended insult. Amateur politicians fail to recognize the difference. They respond or react to accidental offense and purposeful insult (or verbal assault) in the same ways. Accidental offense happens when a person doesn't think before speaking or acting, perhaps because he or she is tired, distracted, impulsive, or misinformed. We all misspeak at times. The proficient politician gives people a chance to reconsider and revise what they've said or done. The following conversation is an example of reacting without thinking.

> Frank: You had a lot to say in the meeting.
> Ned: Better than sitting there like a bump on a log.
> Frank: What do you mean?
> Ned: I'm just saying that someone had to make a move. It sure wasn't going to be you.

Ned quickly assumes that Frank was insulting him and implying that he said too much. This assumption may be correct—but even if it is, what benefit does Ned derive from turning the conversation into a tit-for-tat exchange? Frank's comment could be taken a number of ways, some positive, some negative. Ned is in a position to impose the meaning of his choice. If, for example, he had treated Frank's comment as constructive advice, he might have taken the next approach.

> Frank: You certainly had a lot to say in the meeting.
> Ned: I guess I did hog the floor once or twice.
> Frank: To be honest, I was a little envious. You really made them think.

This approach gives Frank a chance to be positive. It also affords Ned a chance to revise his meaning in a more positive way. Conversations, especially contentious ones, are full of such opportunities. By admitting to having talked quite a bit, Ned doesn't defend himself, as Frank might have expected. If Frank replies by saying "Hog the floor is right!" then Ned will know that Frank really intended to criticize him. But Frank might choose—as in the last conversation—to continue to be positive. It isn't easy to do that in the face of insult, but it can keep a conversation from going completely sour and perhaps taking an important relationship along with it.

The following is an example of how giving someone the chance to do the right thing can be a very profitable conflict resolution strategy. Chris Duncan, a high-level executive at a West Coast paper products company, shared this story with me:

> Our VP of Operations is a twenty-eight-year-old who has a fifty-year-old Director of Engineering reporting to her. There's friction that's constantly building. New product launches get delayed because of it. One time we lost $40,000 on a delivery sixty days late due to admitted foot-dragging by the VP who'd felt "out of the loop" in the product development headed by the director of engineering. I decided to approach the VP to discuss the situation. I really wanted to tell her to get off her high horse and start working with the engineer. But after fifteen minutes of unproductive exchange, I decided upon another tack. I suggested that, as the leader, she could overcome the engineer's weaknesses and find new ways to manage him.
>
> The result was positive. The VP and director of engineering began to work together more effectively simply because the VP's new way of looking at her role allowed her to do the right thing—be a mentor rather than an obstruction.

REVISE THE MEANING OF WHAT WAS SAID

Even in cases where you're sure a colleague intended to insult you and won't change her approach or do the right thing for you or your company, giving her an opportunity to revise her meaning, or helping her do so, can alter situations to your favor. This kind of meaning revision is especially useful in public situations when a direct challenge may be inappropriate or unproductive. Let's say someone interrupts you at a meeting. You might let the offense pass, you might shoot the person a warning look, or you might suggest that you be allowed to finish your comments. If he interrupts you again, especially if you've expressed your displeasure about the first interruption, he is moving into the realm of an intentional affront. At this point, you must take action to halt the behavior. The next example demonstrates a constructive way to revise meaning at a choice point in conversation.

> **Sheryl:** What we really need here is—
>> **Pat:** —what we really need is to talk less and do more. (Second interruption)
> **Sheryl:** You're obviously as concerned as I am about this issue, Pat. *(This is a meaning revision.)*
>> **Pat:** I just don't want our competition to walk all over us while we're sitting here talking.
> **Sheryl:** They'll walk all over us if we don't have a plan in place, so give me five more minutes and we're likely to be ready to move on this. If you can do that, I'll be brief.
>> **Pat:** I can do that.

After Pat's second interruption, it would have been reasonable for Sheryl to abruptly assert "I was talking" or "Let me finish." Instead, she redefined Pat's rudeness as mutual concern, a more positive interpretation. This gave Pat a chance to explain that she was concerned about the competition, not annoyed with Sheryl. This skill of meaning redefinition in conversation is a valuable one. It requires study and practice, but eventually anyone can learn to convert a threatened conversation into a productive one. This can be done by understanding that words are weak vehicles of meaning because (1) most words can be used in a variety of ways and (2) the people speaking them can't be sure that those hearing them will share the same interpretation. Politicians stay on the lookout for moments they can spin the conversation in their favor. If, for example, someone says to you, "You're a little bit slow today," a possible reinterpretation response is "I'm pensive, for sure. This issue is one we can't rush to resolve." Look at the following list. Consider how you might reinterpret the words to produce a more positive meaning.

STATEMENT	REINTERPRETATION
"That's the most ridiculous thing I've heard yet."	"There are elements of seeming absurdity in most innovative ideas."
"Give me a break. We can't take that risk."	"Actually, this is just the break we need to lower risk."
"Have you lost your mind?"	"Lost it? No. But I'm letting my creative side take a crack at this problem—and then I'll go back to the old me we all find so comfortable."

REVISE THE TOPIC BEING DISCUSSED

Topic revision is another redirecting form of constructive politics that involves dropping or diverting attention from a subject likely to lead to conflict. Most people don't use this tactic effectively because they get so caught up in a conversation that they become incapable of managing its course. They respond to anger with anger, annoyance with annoyance. Doing so is only natural, but astute politics requires moving beyond instinct. You need to pause—and consider if replying in kind is to your advantage or whether you should try to redirect the conversation. A short example of how a disparager's own words can be used to change the course of the conversation follows.

> **Mark:** What you just said doesn't make sense.
> **Kate:** Exactly. And it doesn't make sense to the people who work for us either.

Another way to turn a topic around or save it from demise is to ask a question. Instead of jumping to the topic's defense or insisting on remaining on topic, ask a question, agree with some aspect of the answer, and link it back to the main topic.

> **Mark:** What you just said doesn't make sense.
> **Kate:** *(calmly)* Which part?
> **Mark:** Spending money when we're in debt.
> **Kate:** You're right. It's a risk. But it's a calculated one, and I'll tell you why.

Many a great idea has been lost in a premature topic shift, so you need to know how to get back on track when your idea is about to be squashed. Animosity is rarely the way to go. Whenever possible, connect some aspect of the other person's opinion to your own and make that the reason why he or she should hear you out.

REVISE YOUR TONE

Tone revision, like topic revision, constitutes a change of direction, but in this case it involves replacing one tone of voice (e.g., accusing or angry) with a more positive one. To do this, you must be alert not only to what is being said, but also to how it is being said.

Novice politicians tend to ignore tone of voice. Yet being aware of it is critical. When the tone doesn't match the content, observant people become skeptical. When they sense a disconnect between what is said and the way it is said, they are put on guard. It is important to monitor your tone. You can use it for emphasis or to alter a conversation's direction. If you find yourself losing someone's attention, being lectured, admonished, or manipulated, try changing your tone of voice. This change alone can cause the other person to pause and reconsider his or her approach.

I've worked with people whose vocal tones were ineffective. Telling them to pay attention to tone can help, but often that's not enough. Certain phrases that naturally make your tone more emphatic include:

> *Listen to this.*
> *I'll say this again.*
> *The key issue here is—*
> *I'm sticking to my guns on this one.*
> *This is critical.*
> *No way we're going to stop here.*
> *If you don't listen to me on anything else, listen to this.*

These types of phrases put emphasis into voice. There are many others, so find some that work for you. It's helpful to have some ready for moments when someone interrupts or talks over you.

APOLOGIZE

Apologies can be useful as constructive, redirecting responses. Apologies may vary in terms of the extent of expressed remorse, the degree of sincerity, and the amount of blame accepted.[11] It's important to know *how* to apologize. Too much acceptance of blame, for example, can discredit the apologizer in a conversation or in the relationship in general. This is why so many indirect forms of apology exist. Phrases like "I want to apologize," "I guess I owe you an apology," "It looks like an apology is in order," "Sorry I didn't think to do X" and "Sorry that X happened to you" don't accept blame so much as they express some (perhaps inadvertent) contribution to the current unhappy state.

If you believe that an apology is an apology, then you're not thinking like a politician. People who consider themselves of higher status than someone they've offended can appear weak if they apologize. Therefore, higher-status people tend to rely more on indirect apologies. They distance themselves from blame while perhaps expressing some degree of empathy or concern. They might compensate the offended person as a way to avoid shouldering the blame. "I'll make it up to you" and "You'll forget all about this in a few days. I'll see to that" are examples of ways to avoid self-blame. These comments may seem callous, but politicians know that some people create conditions that call for apologies in order to knock the supposed offender down a notch. In such cases, indirect apologies can be quite useful. They allow the alleged offender to express sympathy, empathy, or concern without fully accepting responsibility for an error.

When Iraq prisoners at Abu Ghraib were mistreated by American soldiers in 2004, the news media and committees investigating violations of the Geneva Convention pressed for apologies from President George W. Bush, Secretary of State Donald Rumsfeld, and British prime minister Tony Blair. The latter two were specific in their apologies but neither lingered on the topic, aside from protestations that such violations were un-American and un-British. President Bush shied from an outright apology at first, letting Rumsfeld do the direct apology. Only after intense criticism did Bush eventually offer an indirect apology that shifted blame away from himself, by telling Jordan's King Abdullah: "I was sorry for the humiliation suffered by the Iraqi prisoners."[12] He then attempted to convince Iraqi citizens, families of prisoners, and the world that America was appalled and that the offenders would be brought to justice. Especially in the United States, apologies tend to be associated with weakness and considered antithetical to leadership. There is also fear that apologies can be used in court as admissions of guilt. Polititians use considerable care in formulating statements that sound like apologies but actually are something less. Several days after Bush's remark to King Abdullah, former Senator Newt Gingrich proposed that an apology about the Abu Ghraib torture be made "on behalf of the American people."[13] This type of apology diffuses the blame so that the person stating the apology is one of many and therefore not carrying the entire burden.

Research shows that men and women differ in the ways they apologize.[14] Women use apologies as smoothers in difficult situations. "I'm sorry if I offended you," "Forgive me if I offended you," or "Clearly I wasn't thinking straight when I said that" are such smoothers. They endeavor to calm another person to avoid upset, conflict, or derailment of the conversation. Women are also more inclined to apologize and to take blame. They can hurt their careers if they don't pull themselves out of this kind of dysfunctional communication pattern (DCP). The next conversation demonstrates how apology DCPs place the apologizer in a less powerful position.

> **Fred:** I'd hoped you'd have this project completed long before now.
> **Marie:** I thought you said the completion date was flexible.
> **Fred:** I certainly didn't mean to finish it at your leisure.
> **Marie:** I must have misunderstood.
> **Fred:** Apparently that's the case.
> **Marie:** I'm sorry.
> **Fred:** Then it won't happen again. We'll leave it at that.

Marie apologized too early and too often. Notice that Fred's comments are controlling in nature. Marie's comments relinquish control and allow Fred to place blame on her. Next is how Marie might handle the situation in a more constructive manner.

> **Fred:** I'd hoped you'd have this project completed long before now.
> **Marie:** You made it quite clear that there was considerable flexibility on the completion date.
> **Fred:** That certainly didn't mean finish it at your leisure.
> **Marie:** Next time let's write down a date so there's no confusion.

Marie's last comment sidesteps the blame and moves forward, by focusing on how to avoid future misunderstandings. By doing so she shared control instead of relinquishing it. Women need to be particularly careful to avoid accepting blame. Research has shown that they are more likely to speak in ways that reinforce an image of weakness and lack of conviction. For example, they use more disclaimers (denial of negative intent): "I don't want you to take this the wrong way, but . . ." or "I'm not suggesting that anyone is to blame, but . . ." People using these types of comments are apologizing for their thoughts before they even express them. If overused, these kinds of statements can threaten credibility. Getting to the point more quickly, raising your voice and being heard, learning phrases that capture attention, and dropping disclaimers are ways to ensure that you do not lose credibility. There are enough workplace situations where credibility gets put on the line, especially in highly political organizations or divisions. Why volunteer for additional ones simply by the way you talk?

PARTITION THE ISSUE

Partitioning the issue is another useful constructive control strategy to have at your disposal. Very often contentious conversations consist of multiple issues that can be categorized according to how significant they are to reaching a goal. To avoid being sidetracked, politicians address the most pressing issues or the ones likely to lead to their desired outcome before they do anything else. Issue partitioning sounds like this: "We discussed X the other day and concluded Q, so that's settled. That leaves S and T. Let me start with S because it's the issue that most threatens to divide us. How we resolve S will also affect our options in terms of T." This type of topic–direction management strategy is a useful tool.

It's unwise to try to deal with several issues at once. If an issue is unlikely to facilitate the advancement of a goal or if you don't have enough information to resolve it, putting it on the back burner can be quite effective. Others may ask why you're doing this; explain that the issue will be partially resolved by dealing first with other related issues. Whatever reason you give (and it's important to give a good one), if the potential for conflict is high, it pays to organize what you'll discuss and when.

SEEK ADVICE

Seeking advice from people who expect you to attack them or defend yourself is another on-your-feet response. Although many people find it hard to let someone else be an expert, it's a very useful political strategy. Asking people for advice usually makes them feel good; you also may benefit by getting some useful information. When you seek advice, be sure you actually believe that the advisor has information that might benefit you. Don't pretend to be interested in what he or she thinks, because it will likely show in your face or be obvious in how you speak. This strategy is risky if you're pretending or if people rarely ask each other for help in your company culture. In such cases, use this technique sparingly. Otherwise, your seeking of advice will stand out as false and manipulative.

WHAT TO DO WHEN THINGS GET NASTY

Viciousness is the name of the game in some organizations, where in-groups and out-groups are common. Backbiting, sniping, making others look like fools, tattling, conspiring, and betrayal are all negative forms of politics. The following chart lists a number of negative strategies you might encounter.

> *Diversion* – *Purposefully going round and round an issue rather than addressing it*
> *Revenge* – *Including the best-eaten-cold variety, where you don't see it coming because so much time has passed*
> *Gotcha* – *A common political game in which a person is set up to look bad*
> *Gossip* – *Especially gossip with a self-serving agenda*

Apparent self-disclosure – Acting as if you are sharing
important, secret information so that someone
will reciprocate with secret information of his or her
own

Fogging – Cluttering discussions with irrelevant
information

Lying – Especially if the lie brings harm to another person

Intimidation – Using fear to attain a goal, bullying

Threat – Specifically promising harm if a specific course of
action is taken

Entrapment – Setting up a person for failure or
embarrassment

Debasing humor – Hiding insult behind humor

False gratitude – Appearing to be grateful to someone
for an action they have performed (i.e., pointing out
an error), while intending revenge for that very
action

False obsequiousness – Appearing to be excessively
supportive

ON-YOUR-FEET COMEBACKS

Here are some ways to deal with deviousness. If you can remember
these, you'll be quicker and more effective in responding.

Buying time–Don't dwell on the fact that a destructive tactic has
been attempted, but rather use time to avoid discussion.
> *"That's an interesting idea. I'll need to think about it.
> Let's meet again next week."*
> *"We've accomplished a good deal today. Let's table
> this new idea until we meet again."*

Questioning–Questions aren't used nearly enough during challenging situations. They can be very effective responses to
defensive-destructive strategies.

"Can you tell me how this idea benefits both of us?"

"How committed to that idea are you at this point?"

"What does taking that step mean for the progress we've already made?"

"How does what you're saying now fit with our plan to work cooperatively today?"

Aggressiveness—At times, aggression is the necessary response to an aggressive opponent.

"If you commit to that, I'll have no recourse but to go around you."

"I have proof that you purposely spread a false rumor about me. If you don't rectify the situation, I'll be forced to take action to do so myself."

"I don't want to be the one to tell Paul that we've reached an impasse. Do you?"

Redirecting—Here you direct the conversation away from a potential obstacle.

"This path will take us nowhere, so let's back up a bit to our earlier agreement."

"There are two roads before us here, and one is a dead end."

"That issue is too important to rush through it today."

"As you'd mentioned earlier, our highest priority is X, not Y. We should focus on X."

A shot across the bow—Use this strategy to show that you aren't an easy target.

"It won't help either of us to begin listing each other's mistakes."

"If you'd like to use our valuable time to exchange personal attacks, I'm poised for battle."

"I could remind you of a time when you were in a

similar situation to the one I'm in now. That wouldn't be productive, but it would be fair."

Silence–Sometimes the best response is to say nothing, look pensive, and then suggest another topic.

Humor–When you feel someone has cornered you, humor can level the playing field; mild self-deprecation is one example. Be careful here. Humor considered harmless by one person can be seen as an insult by another.

Dismissive–Disregard the attack and propose a new course.
> *"If we both hold value X, then talking about Y now is premature."*
> *"That's an important consideration for the roll-out phase. Let's bring it up again then."*
> *"We could do what you're suggesting, but let's look at the steps before that."*
> *"Let's put this discussion to rest now. It's clearly a diversion."*

A FEW SUMMARY THOUGHTS

Being adept at advance work and on-your-feet politics is a tall order. If you're going to be in the political big leagues now or someday in the future, such skills are necessary. In fact, they're the key to success at every level. To get yourself off to a strong start, work on a part of this chapter at a time. Study it and restudy it. Start with an area you consider a weakness. Each day try one of the recommended strategies. With regard to advance work, before taking *any* action, consider how others are likely to respond. Form alliances. Consider timing, anticipate detractors, run your thoughts by a trusted colleague, and, in general, put more thought into any steps you'll take than you've done in the past.

Remember, I'm not equating thought with time. Only rarely do we have the luxury of pondering a problem for a long time. The important thing is to give the problem the focus it deserves and to understand how your actions could affect you, others whose relationships you value, and the problem itself. In most cases, you will be able to devote at least some time to considering the potential political fallout of your actions, whether you float a trial balloon or ask additional questions. As one of my wisest advisors told me, "They won't remember how early you were; they'll remember that you got it right."

On-your-feet strategies take practice. You need to see which ones work for you. Try one or two from this chapter. In general, a good shortcut in terms of on-your-feet strategies is this: Next time you're confronted with a dilemma at work, think of what Reginald Strongbrow would do. Then do something different.

CHAPTER FIVE

PERSUASION

WITHOUT THE ABILITY to influence through persuasion, political activity amounts to a lot of wheel spinning. Persuasion is so pervasive in politics that it's hard to know where to begin describing it. An entire series of books could be written on the subject. Because the objective of this book is to give you information today that you can use tomorrow, we'll bypass any in-depth discussion of persuasion theory (which you can find in other books) and go right to "what" to say, "when" and "how."[1]

Political influence in organizations is one of four systems of influence, according to organizational expert Henry Minzberg. The other three are:

System of Authority, which consists of formal power, such as laws or rules

System of Ideology, or the widely accepted norms and beliefs

System of Expertise, which consists of knowledge accepted and sanctioned by formal authority

Minimally and moderately politicized organizations rely largely on systems of authority, ideology, and expertise to function and to bring about change. In organizations that are highly and pathologically politicized, influence occurs largely outside of these systems, or "below the radar." Such influence involves the ability to (1) persuade, (2) manipulate, or (3) coerce.

Persuasion is more up front than playing games. Manipulation often is based on deception, whereas coercion relies on force. Persuasion involves strategies of influence, but people have the choice to reject them; you're simply positioning ideas in ways that encourage other people to adopt them. The quality of your reasoning, evidence, and delivery determine whether they accept or reject your ideas. By contrast, manipulation uses gamesmanship to influence people without them becoming consciously aware of it. There is little or no choice involved because skilled manipulators are adept at utilizing whatever means necessary, perhaps short of coercion or physical intimidation, to make their ideas seem the best.

To become a skilled politician, you must understand how both of these types of influence operate—and how you can use them to bring about change or to protect yourself from manipulators. Let's start with how to become more persuasive. Take a few minutes to answer yes or no to these twelve questions:

ARE YOU PERSUASIVE?

1. Do you know how to make your views interesting to other people?
2. When you are attempting to persuade someone, do you effectively adapt your manner of speaking to the task and type of person with whom you're dealing?
3. Do you have a good sense of how high to set your goals when you are trying to influence someone's thoughts or actions?
4. Can you sense the best time to attempt to change someone's mind on an issue that's important to you?
5. When you've been persuaded of something, do you know what strategies were used?
6. When an important conversation goes off track, do you know how to turn it to your favor?

7. When conflict occurs, can you handle it in ways that advance your cause?
8. Are you conscious of your word choices when attempting to persuade someone?
9. Can you make your most important comments and actions memorable to others?
10. Can you support your ideas with reasons that others find compelling?
11. Do you know how to say no gracefully?
12. Do you know how to use gestures and expressiveness to increase your persuasiveness?

Give yourself 10 points for every yes answer you gave; this will give you an idea of where you stand in terms of persuasion skills. You may have been too hard or too easy on yourself, but if your score was at least 70, you're fairly persuasive already. If you scored 80, you're in the big leagues. Over 90 is off the charts.

Any true test of persuasion skill requires much more than completing a self-report quiz, but I hope this quiz has placed you in a self-assessing mind-set, which you'll want to maintain for the remainder of the chapter. Let's begin with what it means to speak in politically persuasive ways.

SPEAKING POLITICALLY

Is there any other way to speak? Not if you work in a highly or pathologically political organization. A manager attending one of my politics sessions learned this the hard way. Early in his career, occasionally he would notice a close friend and presumably "staunch ally" having lunch or speaking in the halls with his avowed enemy. He dismissed these sightings as aberrations until, one day, he joined a meeting only to find himself on one side of the table and his "ally" and enemy seated beside each other at the other side. The meeting turned into a vicious game of finger-pointing and blame-placing. "I learned more from that incident than any other," this now-senior executive told me. "I left that company. When I started out again, I was more careful. Now I keep my eyes and ears open and stay in the loop. No more trusting people who say they're my friends. I'm a street fighter now."

Trusting relationships can and do exist at work, but those who trust *intelligently* also listen intently to the way things are said. They become students of both verbal and nonverbal language. There are no shortcuts here. Learning to understand what people mean is the most valuable form of knowledge management at work. Easy for you to say, you might think, since you've put thirty years into that kind of study. Luckily you've already put years into observing politics, too—though you may not realize it. I'm going to share with you what I've learned, and you can relate that knowledge to your own experiences.

As I've mentioned, language is an imperfect vehicle of meaning, but it is the only extensive one we have. The words we choose and the ways we use them are functions of our upbringing and our formal and informal education. Consider the phrase "Love is a journey." "Yes, indeed" might be your first reaction, but what does this short phrase *really* mean? That it takes love a long time to develop? That it's unpredictable, perhaps fraught with peril? Is love exciting or arduous? Does it require us to use some sort of map or guide? These and many other interpretations could be derived from these four words, depending on what "journey" means to you when associated with the word "love." We might reasonably ask why compare love to travel at all, rather than to the dawn or a warm, soothing bath. Each image carries a wide variety of meanings of our choosing. Apply this same logic to what you've said today. Imagine how many interpretations might have been derived from even the briefest of statements. Then you see that people are walking around most days thinking you meant one thing when in fact you meant quite another.

People who can choose those words that best convey the image they want to share wield great power. And people who can seem to convey one thought while actually conveying quite another one also wield great power. This is the deep stuff of politics, the "spin" that can be placed on people and events—to their benefit or detriment. Much of political persuasion resides in "mere" word choices. Adept politicians understand this fact; and, unless you wish to be at their mercy, you cannot afford to be oblivious to it.

POLITICAL ADVANTAGE #6

Each of us is at least 75 percent responsible for the way we're treated, because we have the choice to influence what others think and say about us and the obligation to learn how.

If political-speak is taken as reality rather than mere strategy, it's easy to see how the uninitiated become victims. Business can be a hall of mirrors where little is as it seems, and language is the vehicle we must use to make some sense of it. Often the sense-making process itself accords advantage to some and disadvantage to others. However, if you can remember that language is not fact but a means of expression created and interpreted by people, you'll have a distinct advantage over those who believe what they see and hear as if there were only one accurate interpretation.

It's in this sense that we're largely responsible for how others treat us. There are always a myriad of ways to interpret events and to describe them. We can let people put words in our mouths or interpret what we say and do incorrectly, or we can intervene. By failing to do the latter, we abdicate our responsibility to ourselves. Choice is ever present. Why let others label you? Have some input.

I relearned this important lesson in a situation that is a bit unrelated to business—although it certainly affected my work. I was diagnosed with breast cancer at the age of thirty-two. Due to misdiagnoses, it had grown from the small lump I'd found to a much more threatening size as the cancer spread. Immediately many people around me brought that awful disease into their definition of who I was. Before I had a chance to object, someone was assigned to take over my classes. The step was well intentioned, but it was one of many moves by others that pared away at the person I'd worked to become. Then my oncologist sent me to see Bernie Siegel, then a surgeon at Yale Medical Center in New Haven, Connecticut, and founder of Exceptional Cancer Patients, a program of encouragement and support. I'd heard about his meditation techniques and somewhat unorthodox ways of helping cancer patients, such as playing their favorite music during surgery and advising them to take back control of their lives, even from doctors. While everyone else was telling patients what they couldn't do, Bernie told them what they could do. In my case, he asked me what was really bothering me. I mentioned, among other issues, a concern for my career. "Who's making you end your career?" he asked abruptly. I was taken aback. After all, no one was doing that *to* me; the cancer, in my mind, was robbing me of my life. "If you want to work, then work. If you want to achieve, go ahead," Bernie said. In fact, any problem I mentioned to him that first day, he essentially replied with "Why?" or "If you don't want that, then don't accept it. Change it." "If you want children, have them," he said, advice that nearly made my oncologist faint when I told her. What he meant was "Don't let the disease define you. Perhaps children aren't in the picture at this point, but they might be later on, so stop dwelling on that and get on with things. Define your life, beat this damn disease, and do it by taking responsibility." That's what I heard that day and the many days thereafter when I saw Bernie Siegel. To this day I still listen to his empowering tapes. The lesson I learned was that I am the final arbiter of my life, and so are you. Even in the face of seemingly insurmountable odds, you can take back control. Often that means rejecting labels foisted on you and acting in ways that will cause others—and, more important, you yourself—to see you in a positive light.

When it comes to defining yourself and your ideas, the key is not to abdicate responsibility to others who don't deserve the privilege. In the skillful hands of an adept politician, anything can be made to seem like something else. A sow's ear becomes a silk purse, and vice versa. Anyone considering himself a slam-dunk for promotion, for example, had better carefully attend to shifts in prevailing winds of logic and meanings. What's considered a compliment on one day may be seen as an insult on another if the priorities of the company or division shifts. Paying attention to such detail is a complex matter; that is exactly why so many people are not politically sophisticated. Becoming a skilled interpreter of meanings at a number of levels is hard work. Yet that is exactly what it takes to move up from benchwarmer to star.

I've spent many days working with people who by all rights should have reached the top of their organizations but never had gotten there. They've told me about the incompetence of those who were promoted past them. "If that's the kind of person they want running this business, then the hell with them," one said angrily. In time even this man began to see that "they" didn't necessarily want the technically competent person, but rather the more perceptive and political one. That's often the way things are. If you combine technical competence with political savvy, you're less likely to be bypassed by buffoons.

POLITICAL ADVANTAGE #7

Becoming a skilled interpreter of meanings at a number of levels is hard work. Yet that is exactly what it takes to move up from benchwarmer to star.

SPEAKING LIKE THE DUCK

Some years ago communication researcher Gerry Philipson wrote an article entitled "Speaking like a Man in Teamsterville."[2] It is a compelling piece of work because it shows how men in a town he called Teamsterville speak when they want to be understood and respected. This classic article demonstrates how any community has ways of talking that its inhabitants must learn if they want to find jobs, get promoted, get along with others, and even find a spouse.

Organizations are no different from Teamsterville or any other community where ways of speaking emerge. There is an old saying that if it looks like a duck, walks like a duck, and quacks like a duck, it must be a duck. In most organizations, if a person looks, acts, and speaks as if she calls the shots, she probably does. It's wise to know how to speak like a duck when the duck is a person between you and a desired promotion or job assignment. Study other people's quacks and waddles and use them strategically in conversation.

POLITICAL ADVANTAGE #8

You don't need to become a "duck," you just need to be able to communicate with one.

The next example about how this works comes from a computer accessories manager. He told me: "Throughout my career I usually reported to sales and marketing executives. But my boss, the CEO, has a venture capital background. I learned that it makes sense to pitch ideas in the language of finance rather than sales and marketing. What worked before and what works now that I'm at the end of the sales and marketing line are different. When I wanted to attend a training session, my boss was hedging until I put the plan into his language and showed him how it would result in an increase in booking and the bottom line."

Language makes all the difference. You have to think about whom you're talking with and what matters to them. Borrowing from the work of linguist H. P. Grice, logical language includes attention to four categories of talk:

1. *Quantity*—how much should be said
2. *Quality*—reliability of information you're providing
3. *Manner*—the way you talk
4. *Relevance*—appropriateness of information

QUANTITY OF TALK

Quantity of talk is an important consideration in business. At office cocktail parties, for example, you may know from past experience that the less said about work, the better. Or perhaps you'd learned from a parent or mentor that business and pleasure shouldn't be mixed. Therefore, when you find yourself in situations of this type, you should refrain from talking shop. Keep in mind two basic rules when it comes to determining the quantity of information you should share: 1) Make what you have to say as informative as is required (for the current purpose of the exchange), and 2) Don't give more information than is required.[3]

Some people dig themselves a hole at work and then jump in by going on and on about subjects of no interest to the person they're speaking to or of no relevance to the issue at hand. It's important to ask yourself these questions before any conversation: How much does this person want to know? How much should I tell him or her? If so, prioritize your thoughts and present the key ones first. Keep elaboration to a minimum. If the person with whom you're speaking likes to hear backup logic, however, elaboration may be required in order to be persuasive. Here again, though, you always should keep an eye on nonverbal expressions to detect annoyance or boredom. When in doubt, ask, "Would you like me to elaborate further on what I just said?" or "I have some supporting data that I can give you now or send in a memo."

QUALITY OF TALK

Quality of talk refers to the reliability and accuracy of the information in a conversation: not saying what you believe to be false, and not making claims if you lack adequate evidence.

At its best, persuasion is based on truthful, reliable, adequate evidence. People who do their homework (and avoid blurting out an idea before the appropriate and effective time) are more likely to gain a good hearing. Although some people do lie (and as we discussed, civil exchanges require the occasional avoidance of direct truth), trustworthiness is a compelling trait. When people are truthful, they have to spend less effort monitoring their facial expressions and bodily gestures. There is consistency between what they say and how they say it. This is why both truthfulness and strong evidence are so effective in communication.

MANNER OF COMMUNICATION

Manner of communication refers to the way ideas are conveyed. The way ideas are presented facilitates or hinders persuasion in business affairs. As mentioned earlier, many women have a habit of using self-deprecating disclaimers before they speak. "I hope this doesn't offend anyone . . ." or "I don't know if this is completely true, but . . ." are two examples. Repeated use of the phrase "I think" weakens the speaker's credibility. Which is stronger, saying "I think the market is going to grow next year" or saying "The market is going to grow next year"? If you don't have evidence for such an opinion, then don't say it. If you only think something, but don't really believe it, then it's best to not say it at all.

Consider the duck in your organization—the one who calls the shots, that is. Does he act demure, tolerate confusion, respect ambiguity, or encourage outright guesses? If not, no matter what your style normally is, when he says, "Tell me what you think," don't start by saying, "It might not work." Instead, firmly say, "I wouldn't take that route if I were you," or "We're on the right track but some tweaking is needed." When the duck seeks a solution, it doesn't pay to confuse him. If possible, throw him a lifeline. If you're not ready, tell him you have an idea but ask if he can he wait until later in the day, when you'll have it more fully developed.

RELEVANCE OF TALK

Relevance of talk is about the connection of what you say to what has been said before. Being relevant means knowing what the other person is expecting. Have you ever been at a meeting during which someone rambles on, making no apparent connection between what he's saying and what came before? This is a slow career suicide technique. Most people dislike listening to rambling, especially in business where there's often a great deal of time pressure. Grice explains that we expect people to make what they say appropriate to immediate needs.

A boss rushing to the elevator doesn't expect to be pulled aside by someone wanting to discuss a raise. Yet this happens all too often, and it's tantamount to screaming: "I am a political idiot." In all cases, read the cues. Is it the right time and place for a particular discussion? You wouldn't stand up in the middle of an important meeting and ask your colleagues to sponsor your next charity run or buy your daughter's Girl Scout cookies. A senior executive who was amazed at the poor timing of one of his employees told me the charity story. "Who does something like that?" he asked incredulously. "What planet is he from?"

People who walk through the halls of their organizations, coffee cup in hand, dropping into other people's offices to talk should consider the rule of relevance. Instead of asking "Is this a good time?" they launch into whatever topic is on their minds. We now have instant message intruders who drop, no doubt also with coffee cup in hand, into our electronic spaces. "What's new?" they ask, just when you're typing some earth-shattering idea that's just hit you. Once in a while this is fine, but as a habit it's a surefire way to annoy your coworkers. It is better to ask "Is this a good time to talk for a few minutes?" and then really keep it to the few minutes. "Can we meet later for lunch/coffee?" is also fine as an opener. And if someone does have the courtesy to reply to your instant messages, be sure to notice any hints about time pressure and suggest continuing the conversation later.

Before introducing a new subject into a discussion, ask yourself: Is this a subject that should be raised now? Just because it's on your mind doesn't mean you should raise it. Wait until the time is right. Knowing when an issue is relevant to ongoing discussion—what academics call "conversational coherence"—and how to introduce it into discussion—what communication experts call "topicality shifts"—are important abilities. I once had a professor who announced "topicality shift" before changing the subject, but professors can get away with such things in the name of education. Most changes of topic require an appropriate transition or an apology for changing the subject. These considerations are *not* superfluous; they are crucial to advancement in any organization.

GETTING IN TOUCH WITH TYPES OF DUCKS

We each possess a treasure trove of knowledge about how people communicate: rules about who talks to whom, when, why, and for how long. These rules may be flouted or stretched, but they are incredibly useful guidelines. Government officials and their staffs develop protocols, sets of what-to-do-when rules for dealing with other important people. In international relations, knowing country-specific customs, such as how to give the right gift, the right way, is as important as knowing where to stand when visiting a head of state and which flag is which. CEOs of large firms are often blessed with staffs to manage such things. The rest of us must learn on our own how to walk and talk like the duck.

Although categorizing people can lead to errors of judgment, one way to become more attuned to the expectations of significant people is to create a loose categorization scheme. Using the following list, consider how someone senior to you who fits each description might expect you to talk. What kind of rules might apply to working with them?

PERSONALITY	*YOUR RESPONSE*
Forceful	Speak with conviction.
Brusque	Keep comments brief to hold their attention.
Down-to-earth	Make sure your examples and data are practical.
Antsy	They're nervous about details, so provide reassurance, not problems.
Perfectionist	Assure them that all loose ends have been considered and dealt with.

Irascible	Choose your timing carefully before making a request.
Charming	Be capable of enjoying their repartee.
Sensitive	Avoid drawing attention to their shortcomings.
Hands-on	Demonstrate your ability to roll up your sleeves and do what needs to be done.
Insecure	Provide ironclad data about the right way to go; don't focus on feelings.

These are generalizations, so they are not always applicable. It's important to learn what kinds of news people don't like to receive, the kinds of reassurances that influence them, and ways of talking with which they seem most comfortable.

Of course, some people just aren't suited to working together. What if your boss is the type who always talks about her interests and never focuses on you or your ideas? What if he is boisterous and you are shy? Or if he is a liar and you are honest? Even in such cases of mismatch, an astute observer and skillful communicator can find ways to manage the relationship at least for a while. You shouldn't become a liar simply because your boss is one. Rather, ask yourself how you can manage him. Are there ways to keep him at a distance, working with him only when absolutely necessary? Are there ways you can ensure that he won't lie about you or what you've told him? In other words, are there ways you can protect yourself yet still have civil dealings with your boss? If so, then you might be able to work together at least temporarily. If your boss is a real snake in the grass, you'll need to develop a much higher level of self-protection and start coming up with creative ways to change positions as soon as possible.

In the end, with rare exceptions, it is possible to work with and for people quite different from yourself if you endeavor to learn how. Find out what types of approaches and types of reasoning they understand. More times than I can count, I've observed people attempting to convince a boss to do something by providing all the wrong reasons. What matters to him or her? *That's* how you position requests. Don't talk to the duck about what's fair when what she really cares about is profit. An old adage applies here: "Don't try to teach a pig to read. It's a waste of your time and it annoys the pig." Don't appeal to people's moral character when they don't have one. Find out what they care about and make sure what you say is linked to those interests.

HOW MUCH TO ASK FOR—AND WHEN

After assessing the interests and language of someone whom you intend to influence, consider what you can reasonably expect to achieve. Expert persuaders consider whether they want to bring about a temporary, one-time change or whether they want the change to endure. The first kind of change is called *compliance,* the second, *private acceptance.* Compliance is usually easier to achieve, because it merely calls for a short-term change. Getting people to vote in the next election is very different from convincing them to vote in all future ones. If you give them a ride to the voting station and back, gaining their compliance may be easy. Getting them to promise that they will drive themselves to the voting station the next year and in years to come, however, is persuasion of a much greater magnitude.

Most skilled politicians know that to be effective, persuasion requires advance consideration of just how much to ask of others. They know too that if they're unlikely to get what they really desire, then it's wise to consider a gradual approach, where they use smaller requests in ascending order of demand to obtain their ultimate goal. In other words, they know how to divide their goals into manageable steps so that the likelihood of resistance is lowered. I introduced this technique in Chapter 3, but it is useful to revisit it. Here's the incremental approach model once again.

$$A\ 1\ 2\ 3\ 4\ B\ 1\ 2\ 3\ 4\ C$$

Let's say you want to achieve C, but you know it's going to be difficult. Rather than accept defeat, you might consider a goal that is on the way to getting C and easier to obtain. We'll call this B. Between points A, B, and C are still smaller goals. An example of this incremental approach can be explained by using a case I wrote for the *Harvard Business Review*. It's about a young woman who considers sending a memo to the CEO of her company describing the difficulties women in the company face when seeking promotion.

TO: Mr. John Clark, CEO
FROM: Elizabeth C. Ames, Director of Consumer Marketing
DATE: March 8, 1993

I've been working in the marketing department at Vision Software for more than ten years, where I've had my share of challenges and successes. I've enjoyed being part of an interesting and exciting company. Despite my general enthusiasm about the company and my job, however, I was taken aback when I received your memo announcing the resignations of Miriam Blackwell and Susan French, Vision's two most senior women. This is not the first time Vision has lost its highest-ranking women. Just nine months ago, Kathryn Hobbs resigned, and a year before that, it was Susanne LaHaise. The reasons are surprisingly similar: they wanted to "spend more time with their families" or "explore new career directions."

I can't help but detect a disturbing pattern. Why do such capable, conscientious women who have demonstrated intense commitment to their careers suddenly want to change course or spend more time at home? It's a question I've thought long and hard about.

Despite Vision's policies to hire and promote women and your own efforts to recognize and reward women's contributions, the overall atmosphere in this company is one that slowly erodes a woman's sense of worth and place. I believe that top-level women are leaving Vision Software not because they are drawn to other pursuits but because they are tired of struggling against a climate of female failure. Little things that happen daily—things many men don't even notice and women can't help but notice—send subtle messages that women are less important, less talented, less likely to make a difference than their male peers.

Let me try to describe what I mean. I'll start with meetings, which are a way of life at Vision and one of the most devaluing experiences for women. Women are often talked over and interrupted; their ideas never seem to be heard. Last week, I attended a meeting with ten men and one other woman. As soon as the woman started her presentation, several side conversations began. Her presentation skills were excellent, but she couldn't seem to get people's attention. When it was time to take questions, one man said dismissively, "We did something like this a couple of years ago, and it didn't work." She explained how her ideas differed, but the explanation fell on deaf ears. When I tried to give her support by expressing interest, I was interrupted.

But it's not just meetings. There are many things that make women feel unwelcome or unimportant. One department holds its biannual retreats at a country club with a "men only" bar. At the end of the sessions, the men typically hang around at the bar and talk, while the women quietly disappear. Needless to say, important information is often shared during those casual conversations.

Almost every formal meeting is followed by a series of informal ones behind closed doors. Women are rarely invited. Nor are they privy to the discussions before the formal meetings. As a result, they are often less likely to know what the boss has on his mind and therefore less prepared to react.

My female colleagues and I are also subjected to a daily barrage of seemingly innocent comments that belittle women. A coworker of mine recently boasted about how much he respects women, saying, "My wife is the wind beneath my wings. In fact, some people call me Mr. Karen Snyder." The men chuckled; the women didn't. And just last week, a male colleague stood up at 5:30 and jokingly informed a group of us that he would be leaving early: "I have to play mom tonight." Women play mom every night, and it never gets a laugh. In fact, most women try to appear devoid of concern about their families.

Any one of these incidents on its own is a small

thing. But together and in repetition, they are quite powerful. The women at Vision fight to get their ideas heard and to crack the informal channels of information. Their energy goes into keeping up, not getting ahead, until they just don't have any more to give.

I can assure you that my observations are shared by many women in the company. I can only speculate that they were shared by Miriam Blackwell and Susan French.

Vision needs men and women if it is to become the preeminent educational software company. We need to send stronger, clearer signals that men are not the only people who matter. And this kind of change can work only if it starts with strong commitment at the top. That's why I'm writing to you. If I can be of help, please let me know.[4]

In my classes I've asked MBA students to role-play a scenario in which the CEO of Vision Software invited Liz in to discuss the memo. If you found yourself in Liz's situation, what would be your goals? The ultimate one might be for Clark to promise that he will explore the issues described in the memo and make changes immediately. That would be goal C. Rather ambitious, though, isn't it? What if Clark is someone who makes changes slowly? What could you expect to achieve in that case? How might Liz redefine her ultimate goal to be more realistic? What steps would need to be taken en route to this goal?

Ask yourself: How much can I achieve with this CEO, given what I know about him, at this point in time in this company? Which of the achievable goals are also primary ones? Liz states at the end of the memo, "We need to send stronger, clearer signals that men are not the only people who matter. And this kind of change can work only if it starts with a strong commitment at the top." Should this be her goal (C in the incremental approach diagram)? If so, then what are steps A 1–4 and B 1–4? A 1 and 2 may be what she can achieve at this meeting with Clark, for instance, to attract his interest to the problem and to assure him that her description of it is accurate. A 3 and 4 might occur at the same meeting. They could be Clark expressing a desire to make a change in the Vision culture and a discussion of how that might occur. B could then be a commitment on his part to be involved in the change. B 1–3 might identify how those changes would transpire and whom they would involve. C would be agreement on the "clearer and stronger message" to be sent with Clark's guarantee of commitment from the top. Of course, Liz will need to be ready to alter this scenario early on if Clark is not receptive to her ideas and proposals.

This is how politicians think. They assess what they're up against and then identify ways they can achieve change at various points over time (even at various times during a meeting). How well you evaluate the conditions surrounding persuasion attempts influences whether the incremental steps will prove successful. If Liz were a dreamer, she might expect Clark to apologize immediately for the many wrongs Vision has perpetrated upon women, after which he'd go about making immediate corrections. A more realistic Liz would consider Clark's personality, how he'd appear to others if he were to apologize or make rapid changes, the company's culture with regard to change, potential legal issues, and other factors. Then she'd formulate more achievable goals.

The point here is that one of the most important skills of political persuasion is the identification of reasonable goals. Before you attempt to persuade anyone in politically charged situations, you should list your ideal goals and contingency goals. Use the following model to guide you the next time you want to persuade someone to change. First list your primary issue, then an ideal outcome.

ISSUE ONE: _____

    IDEAL OUTCOME: _____

        CONTINGENCY OUTCOME 1: _____

        CONTINGENCY OUTCOME 2: _____

        CONTINGENCY OUTCOME 3: _____

Make sure your ideal outcome isn't unobtainable and choose contingency outcomes that will meet your most important needs. Whenever you are attempting to change what people think or do, it's important to remember that what they *can* do is far more important than what they *should* do. Novice persuaders often forget this, much to their detriment. You should have had juice and bran cereal with low-fat milk for breakfast, but you probably didn't. Why? Because people don't always—in fact, they rarely—do what they should. They do what they think they can get away with, given the constraints on their lives.

Someone who works for you may *want* to get his work done quickly in order to please you but may not be capable of doing so. Perhaps your first step is to find out why. Is he really incompetent, or are there conditions at work (perhaps a training deficit) that make it impossible for him to reach your ideal? Have you set the bar too high? Are there incremental goals you could identify that might help him succeed? This is the kind of thinking that goes into effective persuasion of all kinds, especially political persuasion, where complex conditions surround any attempt to change people.

COMMONLY EMPLOYED PERSUASION STRATEGIES

The fifth question in the persuasion inventory in the beginning of the chapter asked: When you've been persuaded of something, do you know what strategies were used? If you answered affirmatively, you're ahead of most people. There are a myriad of persuasion strategies, though some are more common because they tend to be more effective. Communication expert Robert Cialdini described such strategies in his book, *Influence*.[5]

One such strategy is reciprocity. Politicians don't squander favors. Knowing that most people are influenced by a sense of obligation, they develop favor banks. Cialdini tells of a family, the Harrisons, who decided to test the law of reciprocity by sending Christmas cards to total strangers and then waiting to see if they would receive cards in return. A student in Cialdini's class had gotten one of the cards. The first year she resisted sending a card to the Harrisons, believing that their card had been sent to her family by mistake. The next year, when another card arrived from the Harrisons, she decided to mail a card in return. For years they exchanged cards. She even included notes about her family. Years later her son Skip was accepted into the University of California—Santa Barbara. He needed to arrive on campus a day early and had nowhere to stay. She and her husband wondered whom they might know in Santa Barbara. Lo and behold, they realized they did know one family there—the Harrisons. They wrote and asked if Skip could stay with them. The Harrisons responded with enthusiasm that of course "the Skipster," whom they knew only through years of Christmas card inserts, could stay with them. Such is the power of reciprocity.

Cialdini argues that people often squander this power. They do someone a favor and when appreciation is expressed, they reply: "It was nothing." Instead, Cialdini suggests saying something like "I'm sure you'd do the same for me." This phrase establishes that a favor was indeed given and that one is now owed. But because it does so in an indirect fashion, the intention to commit someone to a future favor is deniable. Still, most people would get the message.

Skilled politicians are more likely to create conditions of obligation in subtle ways. If you know that someone's child is interested in tennis, for example, sending a program from a pro tennis match shows consideration but also can elicit obligation. You thought of my child, so I should think of you or your child and do something in return. This tactic may be in the gray area between persuasion and manipulation, but most skilled politicians would consider it tame by comparison to the kinds of political games played in most organizations.

Hollywood-based freelance writer John Hallenborg considers his failure to hide how easily he completes projects to be a fault he wants to correct as a businessman: "I often honestly say 'no problem' when the client wants to hear otherwise. If there are problems, the difficulties somehow confirm the gravity of the project for the client, and thus the expenditure of the funds allocated to it." And if the client feels that the project fee was too high, then he's likely to record it as a substantial deposit in the favor bank.

Be careful not to become indebted over small issues. Save the big debts for big favors. Be proactive with favors, granting them as a matter of course, often with no intention of calling in a reciprocal favor. One seasoned executive told me he holds aside one hour a week to send thank-you notes and articles of interest to people significant to his work and personal life. Even those people who believe he has a political motive are pleased to hear from him, as he doesn't overdo it.

The use of scarcity is another way that people persuade others to comply. Remember the Beanie Baby craze? Tyco cleverly convinced millions of children and their parents that many of these mass-produced dolls were scarce items. This drove up the prices to ridiculous levels. People want what they can't have, and they are especially interested in things that aren't readily available. This is why you shouldn't always be available to do unimportant tasks. Whenever possible, save your availability for visible, highly prized projects. Being a team player and doing things to help people is admirable, but taking on worthless, time-consuming tasks shouts to the world that you're available, that your time isn't valuable, and that you aren't all that important.

Consider closing your office door on occasion, if this is acceptable in your company's culture (and if you have a door). Put up a note stating when you'll be free again. Don't prance around self-importantly; don't busily rush about. Such actions don't indicate scarcity of time; rather, they suggest arrogance and disorganization. I once watched a new hire rush about the halls of his new organization like a chicken with its head cut off. He'd run in and out of offices because that's the way people had worked in his last job. In his new organization, competence was demonstrated not only by being busy, but also by being calmly so. When we talked, I suggested that he slow down and work on appearing competent rather than panicked. He made the change and people ceased wondering whether he was suited to the job.

Demonstrating authority is another way to enhance your chances of successful persuasion. Effective politicians know how to establish their expertise in areas important to their organizations. Some are niche players—they find an area of growing importance that their company has neglected (or not yet noticed), and they become experts in that field. Or they identify a niche not yet adequately filled and go about making themselves the resident expert. They study the way people in their organizations get the word out about personal accomplishments. Many people use year-end memos reviewing team accomplishments, as well as visible pats on the back at key meetings. Working your way up the project visibility ladder is another way, as is working with people who are willing to promote the successes of others. Don't work for people who want everything you do to be a reflection on them or, worse, who grab the credit. Some people will tell you that your job is to make the boss look good. To a certain extent that may be true, but if the boss has no interest in crediting you publicly for your work, then find another, more generous boss.

In a seminar, I recently talked with a senior manager who told me that he feels uncomfortable advancing himself. His boss is content to let him remain invisible, so he works diligently but with little recognition. When others told him he was on a fast track to oblivion, he appeared flustered. I suggested he keep three things in mind if he expected to advance in his company: visibility, centrality, and relevance. Make your work visible to the right people. Put yourself in positions to be noticed (especially if your boss doesn't credit you publicly)—this is centrality. And be sure your work is relevant to the goals of the organization, especially the more pressing goals.

THE ACE METHOD

It's difficult to remember persuasion strategies if you aren't thinking about them on a regular basis. One shorthand method I've developed is the ACE method. Here is another acronym to store in your memory. Research tells us that three primary types of reasoning persuade people. These are appeals to:

1. *Appropriateness*—what others are doing
2. *Consistency*—what a person like you would do
3. *Effectiveness*—what will get you what you want

The next time you want to persuade someone, ask yourself: What does he or she care about most: being appropriate, consistent, or effective? Then develop your primary approach around the answer to that question. Advertisers do this all the time. They know that flavor is less likely to sell cola than will ads showing people like the target consumer having fun while drinking it. Cars for the younger, less established set need to be similar to other models members of that group are buying, as well as affordable. Expensive cars are more likely to be sold on appeals to appropriateness and consistency—what people in your wealthy peer group (or the one you wish you belonged to) are buying.

Appeals to appropriateness include statements like "Everyone is going to be there" or "Everyone we know is doing it." Appeals to consistency state or imply "Someone like you would do this." Appeals to effectiveness mean "Doing this will get you what you want." Of course, to use the ACE method successfully, you must know how someone thinks. Such knowledge can be very useful. When there's little time for planning before persuasion must take place, this shorthand method can help determine an approach likely to succeed. If you know that someone is not concerned with what others think or do, using social pressure to persuade will likely fail. Similarly, if a person is very focused on her goals, as opposed to what other people think, trying to influence her with comments about what someone like her would do will do little good. Tell her what you think is likely to be effective. That's what she cares about.

Persuasion isn't about what would persuade you; it's about what is likely to persuade others. Astute politicians study how others think; they don't waste their breath appealing to people in ways that don't interest them. The ACE method can help you zero in on what matters most to a person or even a group. Using this method, you funnel decades of persuasion research down to three possible approaches. It isn't a no-miss method, but it sure beats not having one at all.

SAYING AND DOING WHAT'S MEMORABLE

Given the amount of competition most of us face while moving up in organizations, there's much to be said for being remembered when the time comes to determine promotions. A media marketing manager told me that he once made himself memorable by purchasing a new sports car, a model common among upper management in his company at the time. In some companies, that same move might appear too ostentatious, but this manager was sure that what he called this "shallow move" made him stand out when it came time for promotions.

You can make yourself memorable by being helpful at a key moment. Providing novel and effective solutions to problems when others are at a loss, saying something brilliant, or making an impressive comeback despite challenges or setbacks are other ways. Because so many people do only the minimum and others need constant guidance, people who go the distance in finding solutions to problems and who demonstrate admirable independence make themselves valuable.

One of the most effective ways to create memorable messages is by using metaphors. The metaphor is a mysterious form of speech. Scholars have argued about the origins of its power and effect. The best metaphors combine two concepts to yield a meaning more compelling than merely the sum of the parts. Literal meanings can be boring and make people offering them seem long-winded, but skilled politicians know that a metaphor transcends the restrictions of everyday language. In short, metaphors typically provide novel and intriguing ways of looking at a situation. Some of the best metaphors state something that could not possibly be true. When Juliet says to Romeo, "The light that shines comes from thine eyes," she does not literally mean that his eyes are lighting up her chamber. Yet we know what she meant and are pleased by the beauty of her words. They are memorable. John F. Kennedy's "Ich bin ein Berliner" didn't mean he was abdicating his U.S. citizenship or that he'd been born in Berlin. It was a declaration of his solidarity with the citizens of Berlin. Colorful speech has vivacity, a life that reaches out and grabs our attention. When emotion is captured within the metaphor, the force is ever more intense.

Similes are also useful in crafting memorable images. "Leading faculty is like herding cats" is the way a dean might explain defeat to a provost who'd expected more support from professors on a proposed change in teaching schedules. When referring to someone with a domineering personality, the phrase "She cracks the whip like a lion tamer in the circus" leaves little to the imagination.

What does this mean to those of us who communicate with less than Shakespearean eloquence? It means, first, that we should listen at work to see if those people who persuade most effectively do so at times with images rather than long explanations. Do they capture their meanings in colorful, memorable ways? And are you able to try such an approach yourself? Forcing listeners to unravel a seemingly infinite string of metaphors probably won't make a positive impression; metaphors have the most impact when they are reserved for special occasions. So use metaphors, but use them sparingly. Benjamin Franklin had a more memorable way of advising the same: "Everything in moderation."

Stories are another way to influence memory. In childhood we learn stories that remain with us forever. The beginning-middle-and-end structure of stories makes them memorable to adults as well. The public speaker who begins with a good short story draws the audience in irresistibly. If you want people to keep you in their thoughts, develop a repertoire of stories you can use to convey ideas that would be cumbersome and even forgettable if described in another way.

Stories also can be used to get out of difficult situations. Rather than confronting an antagonistic person directly, consider launching into a story relevant to the situation. Borrow this one, for instance. It comes from an attorney who is usually willing to accept novel ideas and to let a better one replace hers. "This reminds me of the young guy who thought he had me cornered. Here I was explaining how we should approach this case, and he interrupts with what he clearly sees as a superior approach. Now, this guy is young enough to be my son, so I'm cutting him some slack even though he worked for me. But then the smug brat goes too far. He looks at everyone else at the meeting and then at me and says, swelling with anticipated victory: 'Sorry, Sharon. It looks like this idea is grabbing everyone so we should go with it.' I nodded but my look told him what he needed to know. He won, but he was gone in less than a month. I guess some of us just don't like public humiliation."

The problem wasn't with the young man's idea; it was his way of introducing it and his apparent need to make Sharon look bad in order to make himself look good. Sharon later used the story to warn a new person who thought he had all the answers that there's a time, a place, and a manner in which to present them. It gave him pause, and that gave him time to learn how to suggest ideas in politically savvy ways.

MANAGING THE COURSE OF CONVERSATION

Persuasion is not only about logic; it's about structure. Conversations have structure. One way to look at conversation structure is in terms of directionality. Each comment a person makes can be identified as one-up, one-down, or one-across in nature.[6] One-up moves, signified by an upward arrow (⇧), are moments when you take control of a conversation. One-down moves, signified by a downward arrow (⇩), occur when you relinquish control. One-across moves, signified by an across arrow (⇨), neither take nor relinquish control. They are neutral. The following conversation illustrates these kinds of moves.

> **Eleanor:** We'll take the steps I just outlined. (⇧)
> **Bill:** I don't agree. (⇧)
> **Eleanor:** The decision was already made. (⇧)
> **Bill:** By you, maybe, but not by the team. (⇧)
> **Eleanor:** You must have been absent for that meeting. (⇧)
> **Bill:** I haven't missed any meetings. (⇧)
> **Eleanor:** Perhaps I was wrong about that. (⇩)
> **Bill:** (Says nothing). (⇨)
> **Eleanor:** But I'm not wrong about the agreement to go forward with those steps. (⇧)
> **Bill:** Given the confusion, I suggest we take a vote. (⇧)

Eleanor takes a decisive stand—a one-up move. Bill counters with a one-up rejection. Then the conversation becomes competitive in terms of control, with Eleanor making the only one-down comment, to which Bill replies with a neutral one-across. Eleanor comes back with a one-up, and Bill does the same.

All conversations are a mix of these three types of moves. When too many one-ups follow in succession, an observant politician recognizes that it may be time for a change before the conversation spirals into a conflict. After Eleanor stated, "The decision was already made," Bill's decision to make a personal attack takes the exchange farther away from his goal. What could he have said at that choice point? As we've discussed, when disagreements arise, questions are often useful. "When was that decision made?" is one option he might have taken. Eleanor might have then replied, "I believe it was at the last meeting." That comment is a one-up but not a strong one. It leaves an opening. Bill could then say, "You're right. We did discuss the steps then. I remember that we were inclined to use them but there was some concern. Arnold, weren't you one of the people who wondered whether they would work?" Here Bill has used the opening to place more doubt in the minds of those listening. Now Arnold is in on the conversation as evidence of a lack of consensus. Bill has done this not by challenging Eleanor, as in the original conversation, but by inquiring (a one-across move).

Because conversations are the building blocks of daily social life, knowing how to manage them is critical to success at work. If you can't manage the directions of your conversations, you put yourself at the mercy of those who can. Turning a heated exchange like the one between Eleanor and Bill into a civil, productive one takes patience and skill. It can be done by avoiding bad habits, such as replying to attacks with immediate counterattacks. Often the best reply is a form of retreat (i.e., a one-down move), followed by an advance along a different route.

Being predictable in conversation is not politically effective. Next time you're in a conversation that isn't going as you'd like, try doing something different. A question might provide you an opening to take a more productive path. Identifying a common ground in the middle of a developing conflict can turn the direction to a more favorable one. After you've given a presentation, if someone raises his hand to angrily challenge something you've said, that is a choice point. Should you argue with this person? Probably not. Instead, find something in what he's said that you agree with. Say "Tell me more about why you disagree," or credit some aspect of his observation before telling him where your ideas diverge. This is how conversations are managed constructively. Try these scenarios for practice.

> *You walk into a meeting and sit down. Someone whom you don't respect says to you, "That comment you made yesterday was off the wall." How might you respond if you wanted to turn the conversation around to a more productive track?*

> *You try convincing your boss to implement an idea. She says, "I don't want to hear it. We're not doing something different now. Forget it."*

On your team, someone who often tries to shift the blame to others when she's done something wrong has just said to you at a meeting, "You fix the latest situation since you're so tight with the boss."

In each of these three scenarios, you might tend to react in anger. It would be an understandable reaction but not a politically wise one. Each scenario places you at a choice point. What could you say or do to achieve your goal while keeping yourself out of a direct conflict? Think of a person in your life like the one in the scenario and what he or she might say to provoke you. Come up with a reply that this person wouldn't expect of you. Your goal is to turn the conversation in your favor. If possible, do it by taking the high ground. You even could find something in what was said that makes sense. In the first scenario, a possible response to someone who considered your comment "off-the-wall" would involve agreeing with your detractor in some way. You might reply, "Yes, my comment was creative, but that's what it takes to solve a complex problem." Here the word "creative" is used as a constructive replacement for "off-the-wall." This kind of redefinition of what was said is a handy strategy.

You could use this kind of strategy in the defensive boss scenario as well. If your boss dismisses one of your ideas, you might say, "I wasn't thinking of something different. What we're doing is absolutely on target. I was thinking of a minor but important embellishment." If that's not your style, consider saying something along the lines of "Different wouldn't be good. But tweaking what's working to make it better might be."

In the third scenario, you might address the comment about you being "tight with the boss" by saying "He does listen to me, but there's a reason for that." Of course, that could irritate your detractor by implying that the boss doesn't listen to her, but on occasion that might not be a bad approach to take. If you want to turn the conversation around to a more constructive track, however, you might say, "I don't mind going with someone else from this team to talk to Sean. You're right. He's good about listening to people who approach him the right way, and I try to do that." This reinterprets "tight with the boss" as being able to speak with him in a way that encourages listening (implication: your detractor can't do this). If she replies with "What do you mean by that smart remark?" you could say, "I think we should put our best foot forward."

USING THE DOMINO EFFECT

Wording is important in delicate communication situations, especially at the early stage, when much is decided about how "poised for battle" each side must be. Good public speakers devote considerable attention and practice to the first few minutes of their remarks. Many impressions are formed in the opening moments—impressions that are unlikely to change easily. Such impressions are created in conversation as well, and the words used early on can make or break progress. It pays to think before you speak.

This brings us to another important consideration. Before the order of issues and points is finalized in a written agenda, consider whether success on any early issue might lead to success on subsequent ones through a sort of *domino effect*. If the other side concedes in one area, concession on related issues might easily follow. Therefore, often it pays to *bundle issues* in terms of background logic. Suppose, for example, that Liz, the marketing director concerned with the way women were treated in her company, can convince the CEO that interruptions and disparaging remarks inhibit women's contributions and progress at Vision Software. She might follow up with a connection to the "men-only" bar, describing it as equally obstructive. If the CEO abhors obstructiveness in his company, any issue that can be bundled into that category might reasonably further Liz's case. Skilled negotiators bundle topics. For example, they may order issues according to their importance, but if they make progress on one major issue that might cast a halo effect on another, they quickly move that related issue to the foreground. Such versatility in agenda formulation develops over time, but even fledgling negotiators can benefit from practice in this area; try developing a flow chart delineating how issues can be bundled depending on where initial progress is made. Here is an example of this issue bundling:[7]

ISSUE ONE: _____

> If the outcome on Issue 1 is _highly cooperative_, then Issue 2 will be: _(priority issue topically related)_
> If the outcome on Issue 1 is _moderately cooperative_, then Issue 2 will be: _(possible move to topically related issue)_
> If the outcome on Issue 1 is _uncooperative_, then Issue 2 will be: _(topically unrelated issue)_

When you're up against especially uncooperative conditions, bundling is unlikely to be useful. Another approach to agenda-setting borrowed from negotiation is to purposely "take a beating" on some issue(s) up front, in hopes that the other side will feel inclined to let you win on a subsequent issue. A union negotiator explained this process to me: "We always sit down beforehand and decide which things we can give away. I might say after giving them what we really didn't need anyway, 'How much more blood are you going to draw from me?' Then they reciprocate."

This tactic may seem another gray area between persuasion and manipulation, but here's the point: You have to give to get in most relationships, and it makes sense to give up on minor issues if it means winning on the big ones.

CHAPTER SIX

POLITICAL POWER

I N HIS 1951 book, *White Collar*, C. Wright Mills candidly disparaged the road to advancement in organizations of that time:

> Now the stress is on agility rather than ability, on "getting along" in a context of associates, superiors, and rules, rather than "getting ahead" across an open market; on who you know rather than what you know; on techniques of self display and the generalized knack of handling people. But the most important single factor is "personality," which commands attention . . . by charm . . . force of character, or . . . demeanor . . .
>
> Accomplishment without personality is unfortunate . . . Personality without industry is undesirable. Getting ahead becomes a continual selling job. . . . You have a product and that product is yourself.[1]

Power as a means of getting ahead ought to be less important than competence, but the fact is that it is at least equally important. And from Mills's description, we can see that this is not a new condition. You can fight it and watch your career suffer, or you can take the advice from this chapter and learn how to deal with it.

The good and often understated news about power is that it is negotiable. You can avoid becoming a victim of power if you take time to consider how you might go about obtaining it in the long or the short term. Title alone is not power, although it may help establish the impression of power. But most power advantages, even status, can be enhanced or diminished. This important view of power suggests that those who don't have power can get it and those who have it can lose it.

Power is gained and lost because of communication—the means by which power is developed, exercised, maintained, diminished, and destroyed. Communication expert Klaus Krippendorf explains that people often become trapped by their perceptions of power balances—perceptions that could change if they would realize that power is not an object, but rather is defined in the course of relating to someone.[2] In other words, if you feel powerless, it is likely because you've allowed someone else to have too much power. Even if someone has a better title than you, it doesn't necessarily follow that he also should hold all the power in the relationship. If you have too little power, it's time to take some back. In this chapter I describe a variety of methods that will help you do so.

As in the last chapter, answer yes or no to the next questions to assess how well you are building a case for your own power.

ASSESSING YOUR POWER

1. Do you study how power is established and used where you work?
2. Do you take steps to establish your credibility with others rather than assuming your work will do it for you?
3. Have you established yourself as the one to go to in terms of specific types of knowledge?
4. Are you skilled at making people feel good about working for or with you?
5. Can you use words in ways that convey a sense of confidence and power?
6. Do you make sure that your energy isn't devoted to small issues?

7. Are you strategic about whom you depend on for appreciation, reward, and so on?
8. Can you tip the balance of power to your favor when it appears that you are the underdog?
9. Do you avoid flaunting power?
10. Do you choose your battles wisely?

Whether you've given yourself a majority of "yes" responses or not, the rest of this chapter should help you raise your power IQ.

BECOMING A STUDENT OF POWER

Let's return for a moment to the view of politicians as sense makers that I described in Chapter 5. Politicians persuade others by creating perspectives that support their arguments. A similar process occurs with the establishment of power. Those who have it got it by crafting impressions. If we agree that human relationships are based less on fact than on perceptions, it follows that power is also brought into existence by skillful management of perceptions. Someone who appears busy and in touch with important people may be doing no more than anyone else and be no more connected. She simply knows how to act in ways that create the *impression* of importance in her organization.

Every situation can be looked at from a variety of perspectives. There's never a single way to make sense of what people do. Skilled politicians know this. So they sell their version of reality. How do they accomplish this? If more people knew, fewer people who don't deserve power would have it. Given how little time most people devote to studying power in their organizations, those who do study power have a considerable advantage. You need to become one of them if you aren't already. Start by assessing your power base, so to speak. The chart on pages 144 and 145 lists five primary avenues to power and examples of strategies to enhance effectiveness in each. Some of the strategies are deceptive; most of them can be made deceptive. In either case, you need to be aware of them and how they can be utilized. As well as building power, they can be used to take power away from you.

Obviously a good many of these means of securing and maintaining power are distasteful. But you need to know they exist and recognize when they're being used to your disadvantage. At times, within the guidelines of your political compass, you may need to use some of them yourself. Many of these strategies are smart rather than devious, if not taken too far.

Coalitions, for example, are not always harmful. Relationships are critical to success. The CEO of a leading health management company told me he doesn't merely attend meetings, he studies who will be there and considers in advance where he'll sit and with whom he'll speak about certain topics. He doesn't let meetings happen to him; he manages what will happen at meetings. This is how the powerful think. They know that power is not given so much as developed and maintained. Powerful people leave very little to chance. First they assess how power is determined, and then they use that information to guide their actions. Let's look at how a few more of these power-crafting and maintenance strategies work.

KEEPING UP APPEARANCES

Do people respect, trust, even admire you? If they do, you have likely made good impressions on them. If they don't, there are ways you can learn to better manage people's perceptions of you.

It pays to ask yourself the extent to which appearances matter where you work. Do those in power dress the part? Do their offices look like they are leaders or followers? Do they have charisma—a kind of attractiveness of appearance, style, humor—that sets them apart? One company I worked with to help smooth change after a merger had a power appearance crisis of sorts. The people from one of the merged companies dressed casually and prided themselves on treating everyone as equals in a team endeavor. Everyone in the other company wore suits and ties, and the quality of those suits

POWER-CRAFTING AND MAINTAINING STRATEGIES

Appearances

- Impression management: Craft your reputation
- Surroundings: Attend to the decor of your office/work area
- Credibility: Aim to get the respect, trust, confidence of your coworkers
- Commitment: Be busy and in-demand, but don't appear overwhelmed
- Charisma: Be charming and humorous
- Value: Link what you do to company/division goals

Relationships

- Attraction: Make people feel good about working with or for you
- Similarity: Be like "the duck" in some important way, or care about what s/he cares about
- Favor bank: Remember the value of reciprocity
- Mentors: Seek out advisors
- Connections: Get to know people in power who can be helpful to your career

Communication

- Information control: Use caution when giving information to others
- Conversation management: Avoid dysfunctional habits, and going off track
- Style management: Adjust your style to facilitate communication
- Open to input: Do more listening than telling
- Facework: Avoid causing other people to lose "face"
- Flexibility: Remain open to creative ways to achieve your goals

Structural Power

- Job status: Assess the power of your position and ask yourself where your career is headed

- Limit access: Be a team player but don't tell everyone everything you're thinking
- Rewarding allies: Be sure to thank people who help you, and remember to help them, too
- Selective availability: Help out, but don't be available all the time

Knowledge Power
- Keep learning: Never stop learning from people at every level of the organization
- Recognize "Regimes of Truth": Identify philosophies that guide choices in your organization and learn to work with or circumvent them
- Be where knowledge emerges: Locate information sources and be around them
- Create knowledge dependence: Find out what areas of expertise those in power look for and learn about them or connect what you do already to their needs

spoke volumes about how power was perceived. The nontie guys and the tie guys were constantly at odds over this. The tie guys saw the nontie guys' casualness as an indicator of a relaxed approach to their work. The casual guys considered formal dress a means of flaunting power and an obvious indication of superficiality. Although dress may seem a surface attribute not worthy of lengthy consideration, in some companies it separates those in power from those without power.[3]

Have you ever considered whether you have a power handshake? I'm not referring to one that breaks the bones of the other person. A power handshake is firm from the elbow to the hand. It's held for a split second, but during that time it's accompanied by direct eye contact. A wimpy handshake implies indecisiveness and low self-esteem. When a handshake is part of a first impression, you don't want to get it wrong. Women should be especially vigilant in developing a strong handshake because they need to offset any impressions of weakness that might be implied by gender. Don't overdo it. Just make sure the handshake is firm and confident and that your hands aren't too moist. (Keep a cotton handkerchief in your pocket and squeeze it to dry your palm. At cocktail parties, place a napkin around your beverage and carry it in your "shaking hand" to keep your palm dry.) Cold hands aren't as bad as moist ones, but there's less you can do about them. The most important things are firmness, direct eye contact, possibly a nod of greeting, and the absence of hesitancy. If you have any doubt about your handshake, practice with someone who knows what to look for when the message you want to send is "I'm confident."

Appearance also means a neat office with careful decoration. Accolades and photos with esteemed persons often grace the walls of those sensitive to the trappings of power. Don't overdo it, though, by putting too many of such photos around or by decorating with expensive desk paraphernalia and furniture when the company has frozen wages. Also consider the degree of warmth and coolness. Is your office inviting or off-putting? Do people come in and sit down, or do they tend to stand in the doorway? What's your preference? If you want people to linger, the office must invite them to do so. If you want them to think you're too busy for lingering, you can say that nonverbally as well. Your decision should take into account company culture. If the people in the executive suites have offices that say "We're all business here," then probably yours shouldn't shout "I have all the time in the world." In such a company, people with too much time on their hands can't possibly seem important or powerful. Remember, scarcity is valued. If you're always available, your time won't appear coveted. If you're never available, however, you'll be out of the information loop. Assess how other people with power manage appearances while still considering the needs of others. If you're too cozy with people, you lose the mystery that also can enhance power. If you're too distant, you can lose connectedness. The line is a fine one sometimes, but it's one that you must carefully consider if you want to send the right power messages.

LINKING WHAT YOU DO TO WHAT MATTERS

Linking your work to what matters to an organization is another area of importance when developing power. In academia, certain journals are held in higher esteem than others. A professor might publish five articles in second-tier journals, but just one in a top-tier journal could be more valuable to his or her credibility. You have to understand, not just assume, how you're being judged. Remember the tendency of organizations to ask for A while rewarding B. Be sure you know what counts, and then make sure a good portion of your work is seen as fitting into those categories. Notice I've used the word "seen." Here again, perception rules.

A former dean of my business school once called me a "cash cow." Calling me any other kind of cow would have been an insult, but in this case, a cash cow was a good cow. After all, the dean was a finance professor. Had he been in strategy, being a cash cow would have still been a compliment but a "rising star" who was increasing enrollment in her courses would have been perhaps even better. Ask yourself: Are you a recognized asset in your particular company? If not, what's holding you back? I'm not talking about objective data that indicate how you affect the bottom line—as important as that is—so much as people's subjective sense that you do. Better still if you can provide both objective and subjective indications of your value. Don't tell yourself that your work is so special it can't be judged like that of others. With rare exceptions, people obtain the liberty to do things other than what's valued by first doing what's valued. People need to know that you are reliable and trustworthy before they'll accept deviations from expectations. Only after you have solidly established that impression can you work outside of those parameters. Doing maverick work without a solid foundation of credibility, however, is not only likely to diminish your power; often it is career suicide.

RELATIONAL POWER

Relationships are another avenue to power. Are you doing what you should in this area? Do you make sure to attend work-related events where you can easily meet people who do have power? Do you do your homework before meeting them so that you'll know their interests and the ways in which your interests intersect? Are you a member of a forward-moving coalition, or are you spending too much time with company critics? In other words, are you seen as a solver of problems or as a creator of problems? If you're the former, you're more likely to be welcomed into the inner circle of those at the top.

Relational power also comes to those who, in important ways, are seen as similar to those with power. Remember when we discussed talking like the duck? Here the focus is on resembling the duck. Even if you don't think you're like him or her in business terms, what about similar outside interests? If both you and the duck play golf, there's a bridge to his or her world. It's a shaky bridge if that's all you have to offer, but having a shared interest is something like having a key to the executive washroom. It gets you in the door, but the rest is up to you. (I won't go any further with that metaphor.) Remember that although being uniquely yourself may be great, in business it's unwise to appear so different from others that you become isolated. When promotion time comes, who will vouch for you if they don't understand you because you seem too foreign, too much of an unknown, too much of a risk?

To help simplify your assessment of what the duck cares about, consider which of these four culture categories your organization falls into.[4]

> *Control culture* – Focus is on rational decision making and
>   cost-benefit analyses of methods and people;
>   impersonal; "either you fit or you don't."
> *Collaborative culture* – Focus is on people-driven decision

making; atmosphere is informal; people work together;
"you're a team player if you're with us."
Competence culture – *Focus is on standards to reach and*
go beyond; work is rigorous with a sense of urgency;
excellence is the goal; "you're either a winner or a loser."
Cultivation culture – *Focus is on catalyzing and*
cultivating growth of people; there's a concern for
fulfilling potential and inspiring success; "you're what
you are becoming."

These are broad categories and, as such, are merely a guide. Consider, though, how you would achieve power in each of these environments—how you'd impress the head duck. In a control culture, your work and your behavior would need to demonstrate a respect for standards, concrete evidence of the practicality and usefulness of what you do, and respect for leadership. In collaborative cultures, the way you and your work contribute to the team is critical, whereas in competence cultures, what matters are defined standards of excellence and an obvious focus on winning. If you're in a cultivation culture, however, continued growth and respect for ideas and the people who have them should be evident in your work and the way you relate to others.

Favor banks are another significant part of relational power. Make sure yours maintains a healthy balance. As we've discussed, obligation is a rule of human behavior. Many people enjoy helping others, but unless you ask for their help or advice, they usually won't seek you out. Ask yourself right now: How can someone at a higher level of power help me with my current project? Give this person a chance to be the teacher. Listen to what he or she has to say. Most people can spot gratuitous flattery, so don't ask unless you really can use the help. But a lot of people out there are never asked to provide the benefit of their experience because too many of us want to appear all-knowing. No one is all-knowing. Each of us needs help now and then. If an added benefit of connecting with someone in power comes with your request, the effort is doubly valuable.

Joining committees that allocate resources can be a road to increased power. It also can be a road to disaster if you make enemies. Overt favoritism is not only unfair, it incurs the wrath of those who feel ill-served. Often resources can be allocated informally. Who wants your time? Are you careful to be sure your favors are not given solely to people you like but also to those who can help you someday? If you're a political purist, this advice may seem distasteful, but human relations are built on reciprocity. Obligation is part of every relationship, so you might as well do it right. Don't be owed only by those who can't help you; that squanders power. Sure, you can help others out simply because you like being helpful, but make sure to assist some people because they can help you.

COMMUNICATION—USING WORDS IN POWERFUL WAYS

Communication is vital to developing power. Daily conversations at work can form the building blocks of eventual power. What you say to other people will help determine whether they view you as powerful or powerless. What you say also will influence whether or how much others will exert themselves to help you. I've coached people who fell off the fast track because they couldn't hold power-enhancing conversations or make power-enhancing comments when it made sense to do so. One woman (a fast-tracker in the fast-track music business) fell off when she became too much of a liability. She had gained attention in her younger years with her intelligent, albeit flippant, comments. Upon reaching senior management level, however, this habit set her on a path of self-destruction. As she told me, "Why should I worry about what they think? I made it to where I am today by saying exactly what's on my mind." "Well, fiddle-dee-dee," I responded. "You're in a new game and the stakes are high." That got her attention. While she tried to learn how to talk with the ducks, it was never easy for her. She was too convinced that she was always right. That blocked her ability to present her ideas so that they would be heard and appreciated. Moreover, she had already turned too many people against her. The best I could do for her was to help her pick up some pieces, patch up a few relationships, and eventually move to a new division where she could start over. She's a technically intelligent, creative person, but power isn't about having the goods—*it's about convincing people you have the goods in ways that don't insult or threaten them.*

By the time I finished coaching this woman, she came to realize that her methods of communicating weren't some crystallized part of her style and identity, but rather a means of conveying her identity and who she wanted to become. Your communication style isn't *you*; it's a vehicle for presenting yourself to others. My sixteen-year-old son has occasionally said, when I've questioned his choice of words: "That's just me, Mom. That's who I am." It isn't who he *is*, any more than any of us are the cars we drive. They may reflect negatively or positively on us, but just as your car is the vehicle to get you where you want to go, communication is the vehicle to get your ideas where you want them to be heard and appreciated. If a warning light on your car were to go on, you'd pay attention. Maybe you'd try to make it to the next service station, but you probably wouldn't set out on a long trip. Why, then, would you neglect the vehicle that can take your ideas—and you—where you want to go at work? Is your warning light on? If so, you'd better pull off the road and get some advice. Are you really listening at work, hearing not only what is said but also what is implied? When there's ambiguity, do you investigate before taking any steps that might put you in peril? Are you an information outsider, and are there things you've done to make it that way? Later in this chapter I'll discuss how to do "communication repair" to ensure that your vehicle to success isn't a jalopy. For now it's important to assess damages and adopt a receptive frame of mind that will help you learn ways to communicate, hear what's really going on, and speak in ways that cause people to listen.

FACE-WORK

Sociologist Erving Goffman wrote that every time we enter into conversations, we put our "face" in jeopardy—in other words, the positive social value we claim for ourselves during a particular contact.[5] In the course of everyday exchanges, people can cause others to lose esteem unless they engage in what Goffman called "face-work." This term refers to types of communication designed to create support or challenge a certain course, and I'll describe them in just a moment. People don't possess their "face"; it resides in the flow of events during an encounter. Face isn't a trait that we carry around; it's socially created in each interaction. If people—even powerful ones—are politically careless and cause others to lose face, often they can look worse than the person they've offended. The German poet Johann Wolfgang von Goethe once said, "You can easily judge the character of a man by how he treats those who can do nothing for him." Keep in mind, however, that even if someone can do nothing for you now, he or she may be in the position to help in the future. If this isn't reason enough to avoid demeaning those below you, remember that such a practice is unwise because these people often can help you in ways you don't realize. They may control resources, information, or expertise, and they're not about to give those things to someone who has made them look bad. Whenever possible, skilled politicians treat people with respect no matter what their position in the organization. The politician's view is: Why make enemies at any level? They may be your undoing one day.

Face-work consists of strategies that avoid threat to your own face or someone else's. Changing a topic to avoid contentiousness, phrasing remarks carefully or ambiguously to avoid affront, and repairing a previous offense are all forms of face-work. One of the more important political strategies you can learn is how to say no in ways that don't threaten the face of the person making the request. Far too many people in business take on tasks they shouldn't merely because they don't know how to say no graciously. Just as many say no but make enemies in the process. Here are some ways to decline graciously:

> *"This sounds very interesting, but I have to decline unless you know a way to get some of these other projects off my desk."*

> *"I truly wish I could say yes, but at this particular time I can't."*

> *"You'd want me to be honest because this project requires someone who can commit time. That's the one thing I don't have right now."*

> *"I want to help. So keep me in mind to help in some other way when I get through with this stuff."*

> *"I gave this a lot of consideration and if I could help I would."*

> *"I wouldn't even consider saying yes if anyone but you had asked. So, if you really want me to help on this, we need to find someone to take on two tasks that are really draining my time."*

Henry Kissinger once revealed that it was his policy to refuse, initially, every invitation or offer of which he was uncertain. Then, if he changed his mind, it was easier to go back and accept the offer or proposal than it would have been to extricate himself from a hasty acquiescence.[6] It's wise to learn to say no, or you'll be forever stuck doing what you don't want to do or trying to exit situations where few gracious exits exist.

Disagreeing with others also requires face-saving strategies. People who don't consider the long-term relationship damage that could come from blunt disagreement usually discover that their careers stall. Here are some ways to disagree in an agreeable fashion:

> *"I agree with what you're saying, but my opinion differs somewhat in what we should do about it."*

> *"Something you said earlier is actually closer to the way I'm looking at this now."*

> *"Do you mind if I ask a question or two about this plan?"* *(lead-in to disagreement)*

> *"We agree on 95 percent of this. It's just that stubborn 5 percent that we need to work out."*

> *"Your reasons are so compelling that I don't see how anyone can disagree, but I do have one concern."*

> *"I now see what you mean and I agree in principle. In practice I have one recommendation."*

All of these are forms of disagreement that avoid insult. They don't take any more time than blatant disagreement, and they go a long way toward protecting relationships. If conveyed sincerely, they tell the other person that you did not intend to offend — in fact, quite the contrary. You're showing respect for his or her ideas, but you also have hesitations, reservations, concerns, divergences, minor alterations, or questions that need to be addressed in order for you to accord the ideas full agreement. In this sense, each of these approaches to disagreement is face-work.

In some cultures, indirectness is the norm. Face-work becomes quite tricky when people from direct cultures communicate with those from indirect ones. Tricky too are situations in which direct and indirect people from the same culture communicate. At some point the direct person is likely to say, "What are you talking about? Would you just say what you mean?" But the indirect person can't, at least not without feeling rude. I've found that just saying "I think what we have here is a cultural difference" or "Our styles are different, so let's meet halfway" can go a long way toward solving the indirect-direct dilemma. This approach is called "metacommunication"—talking about how you're communicating. It identifies communication differences as the reason for an impasse or ambiguity, instead of blaming either person's intention. In this way both people can save face.

Skilled communicators have extensive repertoires of face-saving comments that are useful when someone appears to be offended by prior statements or actions. "If you don't mind, let's back up and see if I've misstated my intentions" is one example, as is "If I seemed abrasive a few moments ago, be assured that it was only due to my determination to make this work—which is a sentiment I know we share." Comments of this nature reposition what has already been said. "I may have spoken too quickly a moment ago. Let me rephrase what I said earlier" works in the same way.

Some people believe these kinds of phrases reveal weakness. But if used sparingly, they are actually expressions of strength. They demonstrate a level of confidence that allows for the occasional admission of error. More important, they can get a conversation or negotiation back on track, which is power—in a soft sense, perhaps, but power nonetheless.

STRUCTURAL POWER

Think about where you fit in the structure of your organization. Part of power resides in position, even if its final arbiter is communication. This rule applies to all status levels. Power expert Jeffrey Pfeffer explained that the exits and replacements of CEOs, for example, often are characterized by political manipulations and power struggles. To pursue their own interests, the people around CEOs form coalitions and make political trade-offs.[7] According to business researchers Albert Cannella Jr. and Wei Shen in their *Academy of Management* journal article: "Because CEO succession has both substantive and symbolic implications for the interests of the parties involved, the choice of CEO successor reflects the outcome of a sociopolitical process—an outcome that is largely determined by the distribution of power among the parties involved."[8]

This is likely why University of Southern California researchers Larry Greiner, Thomas Cummings, and Arvind Bhambri observed that new CEOs commonly make the mistake of starting too early to articulate a long-term vision for the company. As they explain in their study of new CEO successes and failures, "Upon appointment of the CEO, a power vacuum is created, causing uncertainty and anxiety among senior executives." The process of making change requires new CEOs to be "organizers and political orchestrators" who remain open to input from those affected by proposed changes, especially key executives essential to the plan's success. Essentially, you don't want to step on people's toes too early.[9] And a premature vision statement could do just that.

No matter where you look in organizations, power is at issue. CEOs are not the only ones who seek it, and large organizations aren't the only places where it's important.

West Cork pub and café owner John D'Alton, who earlier in life had been a union negotiator, told me a story that was not only humorous but also revealed how much power matters even in the most remote of locations. As a younger man, D'Alton had been a member of a seven-man oil rig crew whose chief needed to be replaced. The job was a demanding and thankless one, with little financial remuneration, plenty of aggravation, lots of petty disputes, and no visibility since the crew was isolated in a remote area. When one of the crew agreed to serve as chief, D'Alton asked him incredulously. "Why did you do it? Why did you volunteer? It's a terrible job! And there's no money." The new chief nodded and smiled. "Yes, but think of the power!"

That's how power is—in the eyes of the beholder. And as D'Alton noted, "It doesn't matter how many people there are below you—power is an issue. All you need is two. This guy had seven. To him that was big time."

It's important to assess your position of power regularly, whether you're one of a hundred or one of two in a division. Are you in a dead-end job or one that provides opportunities? Is your placement, either in your job or on project teams, enhancing or hindering your ability to gain valuable information about the company's directional shifts? Sometimes the most visible position isn't the most powerful one. *Fast Company* magazine described Vernon Jordan as "deal maker extraordinaire and Washington superlawyer." Yet, Jordan chose not to take on a highly visible position in the Clinton administration. Harriet Rubin, contributing editor and author of two books on power, described the situation in this way: "A former White House official told me that Vernon Jordan could have had any job that he wanted in either Clinton administration. But he chose none, because giving up his many board seats for a mind-blowing position alongside the president would not have been an even trade. All of the prestige, the spotlight, and the genuflection of leaders of the world's great nations—what a comedown. Better to be a node of great distinction, tucked securely in the quiet middle of everything."[10]

Positions with power are not always the most visible ones. Most powerful people take on highly visible positions now and then but prefer to develop power by internal, below-the-radar connections. You need to ask where you are on an informal power map. Are you giving below-the-radar power enough attention? Who tells you things you need to know about your organization? Of these people, who might be helpful? Who doesn't give you useful information? What can you do to increase your below-the-radar power?

You need to assess the power structure of your organization. Who went to the same school? Whose children go to the same school? Which people in power work on the same charity, go to the same church, grew up in the same town, share the same interests? Where do you fit in? Can you become connected via one of these routes, perhaps by mentioning in passing your shared school affiliation or sharing your interest in a hobby or sport? Doing these things may seem ridiculous and even beneath you, but people often make connections on the basis of things that have little to do with business. Don't forget to notice if this is the case in your organization. If it is, you'd be wise to give the "how" of power relations some attention and begin making some inroads of your own.

MANAGING YOUR REPUTATION

Among the immutable facts of life, one pertaining to power is that other people will label you. We can't help ourselves. It's how humans make sense of our world. So the rule here is:

POLITICAL ADVANTAGE #9

If you're going to be labeled, you might as well have some input into what that label will be. Your reputation should not be manufactured solely by others but rather crafted with your own skilled assistance.

This process has two prerequisites: (1) a thorough knowledge of your reputation's assets and liabilities and (2) an understanding of how those around you have (and will) affect the way you are perceived. For example, once you realize that you're considered difficult to please—or if some action you're planning could characterize you in that way—you can decide how to tweak or remodel that perception. Occasionally you can do this before someone formulates his or her impression of you. If you know your difficult-to-please reputation is likely to precede you to an important meeting—and if it's going to be a liability there—you might preface your first remarks with a phrase like:

"Please don't mistake my critical eye for a lack of support."

*"By challenging this idea now, we'll be better able to support
    it later."*
*"Someone needs to play the devil's advocate so we'll be ready
    when some real opposition arises."*

All of these phrases clarify that you don't intend to be difficult
merely for the sake of being difficult. They don't apologize for the
way you are; they provide others with a positive interpretation of
your actions.

A good deal of after-the-fact reputation management goes on at
work as well. It's impossible to know in advance of any exchange of
ideas how negative interpretations might develop. Just as you learned
how to persuade someone, you also need to know how to revise the
course of conversations that threaten your reputation. It's best to
make revisions to incorrect statements about you shortly after their
occurrence. People tend to distrust such revisions if they're made too
long after the event. When the political stakes are high, you need to
stay alert and regularly ask yourself: Is this conversation on track? The
following conversation went badly off track for Matt. Alice's impression of him doesn't appear to have been good in the first place, but
his manner of speaking confirms for her that he is no prince.

Matt: I need to talk with you, Alice.
Alice: Sure. I have a few minutes before the meeting.
Matt: There's no way this project can succeed unless
    you're willing to compromise.
Alice: I see. So the failure will be mine and the success
    yours.
Matt: I didn't say that.
Alice: Not in so many words, but you said it nonetheless.

Whatever Matt's intentions, this conversation is in trouble. He
wants Alice to compromise at the upcoming meeting, but she
thinks she's being threatened. If this conversation were to continue
on its current track, this might be the outcome:

Matt: What got your back up today?

Alice: You did.

Matt: It's impossible to deal with you sometimes.

Alice: When things aren't going your way, it's always someone else's fault.

This conversation isn't going well for Matt or Alice, but neither of them is revising impressions. Instead, they're allowing themselves slip into a tit-for-tat dysfunctional communication pattern (DCP). Matt needs to revise the direction by altering Alice's perception of his intentions. This is how he might proceed from the point where Alice said "Not in so many words, but you said it nonetheless":

Matt: You know that I'm no master wordsmith. So let me
try to revise what I said to reflect what I meant.

Alice: Give it a try. I'm willing to listen.

Alice's comment implies that she won't be easily convinced that Matt has a more positive motive than she originally believed, but she'll at least give him another chance. Matt's job is to reconstruct meaning by revising his words. Here is one way he might accomplish this:

Matt: I know I can act like Superman sometimes, but I
really need your support on this project.

Alice: Now, that's a new approach for you—asking for my
help.

Matt: (relaxed smile) Admittedly, asking for help is not my
strong suit.

Alice: Okay, Matt. I'll think about it.

Matt's initial approach reconfirmed Alice's negative impression of him. But he was able to revise this impression by rethinking the way he went about seeking her support. Because people easily cat-egorize others and form expectations based on those categories, changing the course of the conversation in jeopardy involves careful revision of choice and avoidance of DCP traps.

If you think of each conversation as a building block of your reputation, you'll take more care in choosing words. A warning sign should accompany each workplace conversation: CAUTION: REPUTATION IN THE MAKING. That is exactly what business and even personal conversations at work involve. Power can be diminished by short, seemingly uneventful exchanges that go off the mark and leave someone who could affect your future—whether the person is above or below you in rank—with a negative impression. This is why communication experts stress that power is both largely relational and negotiable, provided you pay enough attention to what and how things are said.

SPARING THE REPUTATIONS OF OTHERS

Coincidentally, while I was writing this chapter, an entertainment industry leader told me of a situation he was facing. He and some of his colleagues were soon to demote a peer—a woman who'd held considerable power for many years. "She has it coming," he said. "And she knows it. She's made a lot of visible mistakes and doesn't get along with most people, either above her or working for her." His concern? She still had considerable connections and could make life difficult for them if she thought their efforts to unseat her would publicly indicate her failure. "She wouldn't accept that, so we have to find another way." We discussed how infrequently people consider ways that those persons whose power must be reduced or redirected can be helped to "land on their feet"—to save face so they can go forward. This executive and his colleagues needed an approach that would allow her to exit gracefully, something better than those all-too-frequent announcements about "deciding to spend more time with family."

We discussed what mattered to this woman. Everyone has to move on sometime, but was this premature for her? No more so

---

than for her predecessors, I was told. Had *they* gone on to reputable positions? Indeed, most had. I asked him whether the change, albeit painful, was not really a termination of her career. Here again, he indicated that although she might take the news that way, such an outcome was unlikely. So how could a plan where she would share power be introduced—one that she might find appealing or at least a reasonable bridge to something else? Until that point, she had been excluded from all discussions of the change. Had she caught wind of that? I asked. Was he absolutely sure that a woman with such power remained ignorant about their dealings? Now the executive looked concerned.

"You can't afford to keep her out of the loop any longer," I said. The best type of persuasion takes place when those involved feel they've participated in developing plans for change. Besides the fact that including her was ethical, if they did not include her and just assumed she'd be unwilling to contemplate sharing power, his group was making two serious mistakes: (1) creating a situation where she'd be more ready for them than they were for her, and (2) allowing their untested assumption that she'd reject their plan to guide their long-term actions. We decided that such assumptions would be tested by bringing her into the loop. They'd find ways for her to participate in the plan, one not already completely formulated. Also, proposed changes, where possible, would be linked to ideas she'd advanced in the past or ones she might mention at future meetings to accord her some buy-in. Finally, her power would not be stripped from her, but rather, when possible, reallocated so that she'd still take the lead on matters important to her. This approach would help her save face and discourage her from engaging in the kind of revenge that is born of public insult.

Most power changeovers don't have to be deadly. Rather they need to be planned in such a way that people who once had all the apples in their basket now have some of the apples and a few pears. Doing this takes creative thinking, but it requires no more time than sabotage, and the outcomes tend to be much more positive. Remember, people with power rarely lose all of it, so if you're not convinced that a more ethical approach is the best way to go, consider that this person may get you good someday. Most publicly scorned people find a way to settle the score.

REPUTATION RX

All of us need other people to help us with our reputations. In fact, people who are the most helpful typically accrue power by being so. A phrase I learned recently pertains to the benefit of others singing one's own praises. A friend of mine had complimented an elderly builder on the skill with which he'd constructed the walls of an addition to a house. The builder replied instantly: "Self-praise is no praise, so I'll say nothing." Now, there was a wise man. Whenever possible, let other people construct or enhance your reputation. I advise my negotiation students to provide to the other side, before negotiations, a biographical sketch that describes their accomplishments or to ask someone on their teams to introduce each member except him- or herself. Keep it short, in order to avoid making the other team feel defensively inferior (unless they've provided you a long biographical sketch). If they already know you, then your best opportunity to increase your credibility will come from how organized and prepared you appear, because those attributes suggest competence. Taking notes when appropriate, demonstrating a good recall and understanding of where any prior negotiation left off, and suggesting an agenda all contribute to credibility—an important form of power.[11]

At times reputation is more powerful than it deserves to be. But it's wise to err on the side of the compliment when dealing with people and when constructing your image. Belittling yourself, except occasionally in a humorous vein, is not a good way to develop power. If you deserve what people are saying, then as one wise man told me years ago, when I was reluctant to accept his compliments about a speech I'd just given: "Learn to just say thank you. You've worked for the praise so take it." I've never forgotten that. I'm not suggesting to act full of yourself, but to recognize what you do well and make sure others aren't ignorant of your accomplishments. Try to let someone else toot your horn. When that isn't possible, find out how others in your organization get the word out about their accomplishments. A lawyer told me that the reason why so many women hadn't done well in her firm was their penchant to understate their successes. "When the men here win a case," she said, "they march through the lobby and over to the watercooler to tell all in earshot about it. The women walk through the lobby to their offices, close the door, and pick up the next case on their desks." You don't have to be a watercooler town crier to get credit when it's due. Find another way that works for you. Power comes to those who know their worth and who find a way to let others know too.

THE POWER OF EXPANSIVE KNOWLEDGE

Power expert and philosopher Michel Foucault observed that people are less controlled by naked violence or the economic power of bosses and landlords than they are by pronouncements of so-called experts, organized into what he calls "regimes of truth"—sets of understandings that legitimate social attitudes and practice.[12] "Regimes of truth" is a term that can be applied to organizations where certain types of knowledge are esteemed, others disparaged, in order to keep power in the hands of those who already possess it. If you plan to survive in this type of organization, you need to be part of the in group or beat them at their own game. Beating them calls for knowing what in-group members say they know better than they know it themselves.

You can't learn this talent in most business schools, which tend to focus on technical knowledge at the expense of practical and emancipatory (mind-expanding) knowledge. Skilled politicians know that such a focus is too limiting. Besides engaging in objective forms of knowledge and subjective forms usually conveyed by stories, it's also necessary to engage in reflective, emancipatory thinking—in other words, wisdom born of critical thinking about the meaning and value of experience. Doing this calls for disciplining the mind to avoid believing that "knowing your stuff" involves technical skills only. Michael Lissack and Kurt Richardson argue that MBAs are "shortchanged" by the lack of emphasis in business schools on practical and emancipatory thinking.[13] This gap in learning is, Lissack and Richardson argue, one possible reason for the lapse in business ethics we've witnessed in the last decade. Knowledge without consideration of how to apply it to real work situations prevents many businesspeople from learning how politics works. Political thinking requires practical consideration and critical evaluation of the pros and cons of all possible courses of action. Much of what you'll learn in most business schools has little to do with political thinking.

POLITICAL ADVANTAGE #10

An ability to learn from others, to listen to their stories and discover how technical knowledge merges with practical and evaluative knowledge, is indispensable to gaining political power.

Can anyone really learn leadership simply by reading a book? No. They can learn *about* leadership, and that is valuable, but they can learn how to lead only by attempting it, by observing it directly, or by hearing the stories of other people. Can accounting or any other supposedly objective activity operate in a vacuum? Nope. These skills are learned only by exposing yourself to the broader thinking of senior people who've already learned the hard way or by obtaining this knowledge from firsthand experience. So if you think that an MBA degree or business school Ph.D. indicates knowledge *of* the workings of business, think again. Degrees indicate knowledge *about* business; that falls short of what's needed to have power in organizations.

Jean Lipman-Blumen, coauthor with Harold Leavitt of *Hot*

Groups—a book about high-performance teams—says future leaders will be those "who want to be where meaning might emerge, the people who refuse to drink continuously from the same information well."[14] So many people who've drunk from a communal well have sat in my office struggling to understand why, despite their intelligence, they've had such difficulty advancing. They usually regale me with stories of the stupidity of those around them. It doesn't occur to many of them that they might be the ignorant ones—at least in terms of practical and emancipatory knowledge. They "know their stuff," but in many cases their stuff is the same as everyone else's.

Drink instead from the knowledge wells of people who are succeeding in your organization. You don't have to do all that they do, but learn how they do it. Keep firmly in mind the fact that superior technical knowledge is a tremendous asset, but it is only one of many assets needed to function in the complex political world that is business.

MANAGE DEPENDENCY

When I first joined the Marshall School of Business, I taught in business communication, an area little esteemed by some of those who would one day determine whether I would be promoted. I published in leading communication journals, but they were not the ones many business professors read. I had strong teacher ratings, which were helpful but not enough. I knew I would never gain promotion and tenure by remaining an enigma. Yet insisting that journals in my field were just as good as those respected by finance professors or complaining that promotion criteria were skewed and unfair would not have helped. What I needed to do was raise my value to the Marshall School. To do so, I was determined to publish in the *Harvard Business Review* and other leading business journals, to obtain grants, to write interesting and useful books that received valued publicity, and to develop a course in negotiation. Over time, the course became one of the school's most in-demand courses. It also pulled in students from all areas of the business school and beyond. That's how I became a "cash cow," as I mentioned earlier. My moves were directed at creating value for the school, and they succeeded. I don't remember consciously saying to myself, "I will now go about creating power." I merely compared what was valued at the time in business schools to what I was doing. Senior colleagues were helpful. They shared with me the views of those in charge and provided valuable advice and support. I continued to do my research, teach, and publish, but with considerable focus on ways that were valuable to a business school and therefore would make all the difference in terms of promotion. These actions also allowed me to continue my research in more tangential areas because those in power were satisfied with the main thrust of my work.

Making yourself valuable is a way of reducing your dependence on other people. Dependence lessens power. If you expect someone to expend valuable political capital for you so that you can obtain a promotion, you're putting a lot of your apples in one, possible shaky basket. The more you can do to lessen such dependence, the better your chances of getting what you're after.

The following equation illustrates the relationship between power and dependence:

$$\text{Power A/B} = \text{Dependence B/A}$$

The power of person A over B is, according to this equation, equal to the dependence of person B on A.[15] Based on this view of power, you would do well to make sure that important people depend on you for some valued resource.

USE THE POWER OF PEOPLE YOU KNOW

"It's not what you know, it's who you know" is an old saw that many of us learn early in life. Yet as a form of power, it's all too often ignored, perhaps because using someone else's power to bolster your own may seem somehow unethical.

Connections can be squandered if you don't understand when or how to use them. Don't drop names awkwardly and prematurely. "I was with the senior vice president the other day and he said . . ." may be an effective call on authority if you're negotiating with an obstinate person, but it may be too heavy-handed if the other person perceives it as bullying, or if he dislikes the senior VP. Before citing your support from another party, it's important to discern whether that person is highly regarded by the other side. (You also want to be sure that you actually do have the person's support. The other side may well check on that.) And you want to phrase your name-dropping in a way that doesn't appear to be contrived intimidation. Be subtle when implying connections; for instance, wait until the subject under discussion relates either to the topic for which you have the connection's support or to the connection personally. "Before last week, I saw that issue differently. But some things Bill Adams told me over lunch have caused me to change my view." This statement doesn't suggest that Adams is strongly on your side. Rather it creates the impression that, without any knowledge that the conversation now taking place would occur, you and Adams happened to discuss the topic now under consideration. The novice is more likely to say something like "Knowing you and I were going to meet, I went to see Bill Adams last week." Such an approach typically results in the other side feeling trapped, and that is not good. After all, people who feel cornered become defensive, and such defensiveness rarely helps bring about a positive outcome.

CAUTION! DON'T FLAUNT POWER

Now that we've looked at types of power, allow me to offer a few words of caution regarding its use. Power does not necessarily accrue to the person with the right answers—or even the best ones. Indeed, people often respond better to those who appear to have some faults. Act as if you have all the right answers, and often others will do what they can to prevent you from achieving your goals. Dakota State University business professor Robert Lahm explains how one recruiter described the way a candidate he sent out to be interviewed acted too powerful, commanding, and knowledgeable about what to do and whom to see. The recruiter advised job candidates instead to make an interviewer comfortable and to avoid frightening him or her away. "And that's what a lot of people do," the recruiter said. "And that's why you so often have employers say they didn't hire because the guy was overqualified."[16]

In the same study, another recruiter described a certain type of salesperson who is just too slick, too authoritative, and unable to exercise restraint: "You get salespeople coming in who . . . had the qualifications on a piece of paper, you know, they had the sales training, they had the record of sales success in prior jobs, they were good looking, they dressed right, they were articulate and all, but what some of them tended to do is, they would come in and lean back in the chair and just try to give you this relaxed, casual, confident arrogance. 'You've got to have me,' you know, 'I'm so slick.' And there was just something about that that turned me off. . . ."[17]

So, while confidence is good, arrogance is not. There is a fine line between the two, but it's one that skilled politicians identify. They know how much to say about their accomplishments. They know how to make other people comfortable while also appearing impressed. Confidence doesn't mean listing the great things you've done. It's conveyed in large part by body language. In the same research study by Lahm, a recruiter described how credibility looks in an interview: "Somebody that's leaning forward in their chair, for instance, and really looking you in the eye and listening to what you have to say and offering valid information, whether you're talking about employment or anything else, you're always getting the feeling this person is listening and observing and that helps build credibility and chemistry."[18]

A good rule is to listen to how the other people in your organization provide information about their accomplishments. See if you can identify someone who overdoes it and then someone who seems quite skilled. What are the differences between the two? Locate others who are also skilled and find similarities in the way they brag and exert or exude power. Methods vary a great deal across organizations; only by studying the one you're in will you be able to find the thin line between confidence and arrogance.

A second rule is to suit your expressions of power and influence to the needs at hand. For example, if a project is in need of a jump-start or a way around a serious problem, you might say, "I could speak to X about this. I'll see him tomorrow." Here the primary message is "I have a solution to our problem," not "I have all the answers." However, your connection to X will be noted. If X is a powerful, highly regarded person, you will have demonstrated power by connection without having to flaunt it. Another way is to say "Do you think X might have some ideas about how to help us?" If the answer is affirmative, you can mention that you'll be meeting him the next day and you'd be glad to ask for his assistance.

CAUTION! USE THREATS ONLY AS A LAST RESORT

The skilled politician realizes that success in organizations is largely about social influence, not about fear. My brother, a (now-retired) submarine captain who received impressive accolades as a commander, once told me that even commanders have to sleep at night. He meant that making people fear you by acting like Captain Bligh does not encourage loyalty or respect. If you don't want your submarine to run aground while you sleep, you'd better know how the people who work for you think. There is no such thing as an environment so command and control oriented that people don't need to feel that their concerns are noted and duly considered. Research shows that subcultures often evolve when people feel threatened. A shared identity of oppression emerges, and cohesive groups form with members looking out for each other's interests. Even if a true rebellion doesn't occur, daily scams may be perpetuated on those who supposedly are more powerful—scams that eventually undermine all that they do.[19]

People may bow for a time to heartless oppression, but they will not do so without dissenting in one form or another. The politically wise, no matter their status, learn to ask questions, assess, comprehend, and demonstrate that they are listening and taking concerns into consideration. Then when they really need to issue a directive, they're more likely to find that their followers willingly accommodate them.

An expert negotiator who visited one of my MBA classes advised the students, "In situations of no choice, *find* a choice rather than threaten." She attributes much of her own success to doing just that. She recommends asking advisory questions of resistant people rather than cornering them. This way, she says, "they educate themselves with the answers." So rather than threaten, ask for information. See if you can bring others to see your point of view, but also listen to theirs. Ask hypothetical questions, such as "What will happen if we don't find a point of agreement? Who benefits?" The hoped-for answer is "No one benefits." Another approach is to ask "How do you think the people depending on us are going to react if you and I can't work this out?" Or "What will you do if we don't find a solution?" and then perhaps "Is that ideal?" My guest recommended, "If questions don't work, try explaining to them what you'll do or be forced to do if the situation doesn't improve." "Hiss rather than bite" is her preferred method of dealing with the most resistant of people. Even they can be reached, she believes, if you know how to approach them. "Phrase what you say as a warning about what might ensue rather than a threat. Saying 'If we don't do X, then we'll all face Y' is better than blaming or threatening."

Research indicates that negotiators who use cooperative strategies more frequently have higher joint gains than those who don't. Those who rely on such competitive strategies as demands and threats fail to achieve optimal outcomes.[20] Threats are acts of desperation, and desperation does not demonstrate power.

On rare occasions when reason does not work, where the people involved are clearly used to commanding others to do their bidding, politicians may use veiled threats. A veiled threat is subtle and deniable. Sometimes it takes the form of a simple reference to a powerful acquaintance the other side does not wish to offend: "I was speaking to Tyrone the other day about just this matter. He told me you'd see things this way as well." If you're negotiating with a superior who is resisting something important to you, you might say, "We could go together to speak with Amanda (his superior) to see what she thinks" or "Since this move could be controversial, would you go with me to Amanda's office so we can get her opinion?" Some bosses find such suggestions offensive, and with good reason. One pronounced risk to this approach is that your superior might go straight to Amanda himself and attempt to create such an unfavorable impression of you or your request that it undermines your approach. If you use this tactic, be sure that the two of you *together* can see the other party right away.

Do you remember the ACE model of persuasive techniques I described in Chapter 5? Veiled threats also can take the form of appeals to appropriateness (what others will think). For example, "Since everyone else on this project wants to take a different approach, we could face considerable outrage or even defection from our team to that of a competitor." This appeals to what others are thinking and warns of destructive actions that might follow a particular course of action. A consistency appeal could be used with someone who cares more about how an action will violate positive self-perceptions more than he or she cares about what others think. "It's not like you to take such a risk without considering all the potential consequences" is a consistency appeal. Finally, effectiveness appeals pertain to outcomes. Veiled threats suggest that negative outcomes are likely. Present the other side with a hypothetical scenario in this way: "Let's say we go down this road. We take what you insist is the best approach, and we discover that our competitor uses the approach I've just described. I don't know whether I could justify continuing this venture."

POLITICAL ADVANTAGE #11

The less personal the veiled threat, the better. To use a dental analogy, you don't want to hit a nerve when you only intended to fill a tooth.

CAUTION! DON'T PLAY THE SAME POWER HAND TOO OFTEN

In my early years of studying power and politics, I was fortunate to have a colleague who was proficient at both. His one fault? He repeated his power strategies and made himself predictable. At the beginning of meetings, he often declined to support a proposal advanced by one of the faculty. Considerable time would then be allocated to persuading him. He would continue to resist as pleasantly as possible. Then, when all seemed lost, when there were no persuasion strategies left, he would agree to go along with the proposal. Great rejoicing usually followed, as if he were the prodigal son. One day I'd had enough. As he passed by my office I asked, "When are you going to stop doing what you did today at the meeting?" He looked puzzled, innocent. I waited. "Okay," he said, "I'll just have to find another tactic." And he did; in fact, many more. He was a wonderful study. Eventually, however, his tendency to repeat even these new tactics caught up with him. When people discover they've been manipulated, they're seldom happy or quick to forgive.

If you use a power tactic more than once, be sure it's not obvious. You don't want to gain a reputation as a one-trick pony. The other side will surely attempt to take advantage of your lack of versatility. You will be seen as predictable and thus easy to win over. Perhaps worse, you'll be seen as manipulative, and that creates enemies. Besides, you have much to gain from having a repertoire of political strategies. Then you can be a person of mystery, someone interesting whom people cannot easily categorize.

Robert Greene, author of *Power*, describes the hazard of such predictability:

> Do not imagine that to create an air of mystery you have to be grand and awe-inspiring. Mystery that is woven into your day-to-day demeanor, and is subtle, has that much more power to fascinate and attract attention. Remember: Most people are upfront, can be read like an open book, take little care to control their words or image, and are

hopelessly predictable. By simply holding back, keeping silent, occasionally uttering ambiguous phrases, deliberately appearing inconsistent, and acting odd in the subtlest of ways, you will emanate an aura of mystery. The people around you will then magnify that aura by constantly trying to interpret you.[21]

If your reputation (in a highly positive sense) does not precede you, then you wouldn't want to take such mystery too far. Contrived mystery works best for people held in high esteem — especially people whose reputation indicates they are so intelligent that others expect them to be difficult to understand. The important point to remember is that anything that makes you easy to read or easy to predict reduces your power. Using the same power strategies over and over is one way to give others a distinct advantage over you — the ability to predict and therefore to manage you. Think about what you can do today to make yourself a bit more mysterious.

CHAPTER SEVEN

POLITICAL COURAGE
AND SUICIDE

In whatever arena of life one may meet the challenge of courage, whatever may be the sacrifices he faces if he follows his conscience—the loss of his friends, his fortune, his contentment, even the esteem of his fellow men—each man must decide for himself the course he will follow. The stories of past courage can define that ingredient—they can teach, they can offer hope, they can provide inspiration. But they cannot supply courage itself. For this, each man must look into his own soul.

—John F. Kennedy, *Profiles in Courage*

A S THE COWARDLY lion in the *Wizard of Oz* learned, we all know on some level that there is no respect in the jungle without courage and no true leadership in the absence of either. The lion ultimately found courage where John F. Kennedy advised us to look—within himself. For many of us, although courage resides within, awaiting recognition, political conditions conspire to stifle its expression. This suppression is especially evident in highly political and pathologically political arenas. Yet it is also from these environments of perniciousness that courage often emerges.

Taking a moral stance in a highly moral organization is not politically courageous; it is admirable but not risky. Taking such a stance in a highly political or corrupt environment, however, is politically courageous. The risks are high because prevailing wisdom or policies stand in opposition. Where silence is the norm, often courage is a willingness to speak up. Where singing the same tune is expected, silence itself can be courageous. Political courage can be elicited by moral concerns, but also by a threat to a worthy personal or organizational goal. Stories abound of people who stuck their necks out or went against the grain only to be assigned a dead-end project or edged out altogether. Given such risks, courage at work may seem ill-advised, but research indicates otherwise. Even in organizations where silent assent pervades, visibility is usually rewarded more than quietude and cowardice.

Yet even those who have the ability to be courageous learn early that it can be quite risky. We begin our first jobs full of enthusiastic optimism. We expect to find people wanting to hear what we have to say, as they did in school and college. Steve Harcourt, senior executive at a leading sport products company, learned this early. As he describes it, as a young man he thought he'd been hired "to get all the money possible—to make a huge profit for the company." When Harcourt insulted one of the CEO's favorite senior vice presidents by suggesting that he do a few things differently, the response was not positive. Harcourt was edged out for a while. The CEO never said anything directly to him, but Harcourt got the message. He now believes, "If you ignore politics and make someone above you look bad, you're going to have a short career." He rarely sticks his neck out now and is criticized by some for being a "political animal" in his efforts to please those at senior levels. But better a political animal, he reasons, than political roadkill. From daily slights and defeats of the kind Harcourt experienced, we learn that standing up to power is dangerous. Courage, we might begin to think, seems a form of naïveté or ignorance. And so the common choice is to give up and to stay below the radar.

But others set about learning the ways of the powerful. They find routes around or through power. In time, they learn the terrain and the intellectual and emotional equipment needed to traverse it.

For them political suicide becomes less and less likely. These fortunate people learn that courage, contrary to popular wisdom, is not spontaneous. In my thirty years of studying persuasion, of which politics is a significant part, I've learned that courage may be boldly expressed—it might involve threatening to resign or posing a challenge to senior management. But in all cases, the decision to be courageous must involve careful calculation. The purpose of political courage is victory, not destruction of yourself or others. And so consideration of options and strategies of implementation is just as critical in courage as in any form of persuasion.

For years I've taught negotiation—a process that, like politics, is dependent on persuasion. Effective negotiators think in terms of persuasion contingencies—goals to fall back on if the primary one isn't met. They also come up with a BATNA (best alternative to negotiated agreement) that addresses what they'll do if a particular negotiation doesn't work out. Having a sense of how much to give and what can be compromised keeps people from giving away the farm, so to speak. Contingencies and BATNAs are safety nets that lower the odds of losing. In politics, courage requires having something similar. First, you need a WO1 (win option 1)—the primary goal. Behind these are WO2 and WO3 and so on, as required. These win options address the question of what to do if events begin to go south. The astute politician also identifies NWOs (no-win options) that address what to do if win options become unattainable. Often NWOs take the form of other ways to come at an issue (e.g., pulling back to fight another day, using a different approach, or seeking to acquire a related goal that eventually may lead to reaching the current one). If you haven't identified win options and no-win options before you leave your office to do battle, then you're surely en route to political suicide rather than political courage. Why omit this step and risk squandering something important to you? Instead, you should think in terms of what-ifs and have in your mind conditions that will signal when one option isn't working and another should be tried. A highly successful international business advisor once told me, "I always go in knowing my ultimate goal, but I know my benchmarks as well." He is a man who is relentlessly patient when he can be, inconspicuously agile at all times, and conspicuously ruthless only when he must be. He told me, and I'd say it's true, "I always win one way or the other."

Advance planning may seem anathema to courage, which we often consider impetuous. But precourage planning need not be long term. Once you've learned to consider win options and no-win options before jumping feetfirst into conflict, identifying them can take very little time. Astute politicians learn to think in terms of win options and no-win options, and eventually doing so becomes second nature. Knowing what might prove to be an obstacle is critical to informed courage. So too is knowing how to go around, through, over, or under these roadblocks.

Few among us won't be called on someday to be courageous. We can shirk from the responsibility or embrace it. If the latter course appeals, then the next step is to learn what courage at work is, when it's appropriate, and how it is most effectively expressed.

WHAT IT MEANS TO BE POLITICALLY COURAGEOUS

Courage in business does not require us to place our lives in jeopardy, as battlefield heroes do. Yet courage in the workplace can be admirable, as it requires stepping outside the norm and facing potential rejection, ridicule, and damage to oneself or one's career in the name of a good cause. Most examples of courage in business are not about increasing shareholder wealth. They're about doing what is right, which is the closest thing to bravery business affords.

Courage is a kind of power akin to but more substantial than charisma. Courageous people are at once admired and feared, largely because they appear to lack fear themselves and also because they are unpredictable. These attributes make them an anomaly. As one manager told me after standing up to a superior who was clearly in the wrong, "People occasionally stop by and say things like 'No one will mess with you anymore. I sure know I won't.'" There's a certain admiration in comments like this.

Courage compels respect and attention no matter how small the act, no matter how well supported. As Thomas Jefferson once said, "One man with courage is a majority."

This kind of individual courage was attributed to Libyan president Muammar Qaddafi when, in 2004, he surprised the world with the announcement that his country, after thirty-five years of hostility toward the West, would be renouncing terrorism and abandoning the development of weapons of mass destruction. He blamed himself and his country for driving a wedge between themselves and the rest of the world. "No one separated Libya from the world community," he said. "Libya voluntarily separated itself from others. . . . No one has imposed sanctions on us or punished us. We have punished ourselves."[1]

Qaddafi explained that his country had done these things to help both African nations as they were breaking away from colonial powers and the Palestinians, but because relations between Palestinian president Yasir Arafat and the White House had improved, Qaddafi reasoned, "We cannot be more Palestinian than the Palestinians themselves." So he offered to shake hands with people he'd spent nearly a lifetime viewing as his enemies. Impressed U.S. senators and representatives praised Qaddafi's political courage; they know, some all too well, how difficult it is to admit to error and to change course.

It was political courage of a different sort that caused Jennifer Morrisscy to leave her company and to go one step further—she sent its leaders a five-page memo explaining why. As an engineer for a leading computer products company, Morrissey saw the contradictions between company policy and day-to-day communication. She observed differential treatment of women that was destructive to their careers. She experienced fear of retaliation when seeking other women out in the hallway, and she avoided any appearance of uniting with them. Eventually she realized that she was living a life of fear and frustration, one she articulated in the memo that changed her company's culture. Why did she send a memo that might negatively influence her future job opportunities? She wanted to help other women and the managers she left behind generate solutions. One sentence summarizes much of what was contained in the five pages: "I found that moving up in the system meant you got to be ignored by a higher class of men."

Although we might criticize her method and argue that she should have stayed to help ensure that the change process would be a success, Morrissey saw things differently. By leaving, she clearly expressed the seriousness of the situation. She told me that she might have stayed and coped if she'd developed a network earlier on in her career, but under the circumstances, her departure was the best way to make a point. She opened herself up to the kind of disparagement and derogatory labeling that women fear because she wanted to make a difference. The company benefited because the CEO and some senior managers decided not to ignore her warning. Rather than attack the messenger, they revised their company. That too was courageous.[2]

Sometimes courage is the product of personal philosophy. A much sought-after French Management Development consultant shared with me that one of her clients told her that she would likely never become a millionaire because she refuses to work with her customers' competitors. Additionally, unlike most consultants, she visits companies before agreeing to work with them. She pays for her own travel and stays for two days "interviewing whoever I like," she explains, all at her own expense. She asks herself: "Do I respect their values? Are they too political? Can I commit my heart and mind to their product? Will I bring real added value? Do I fit in the company culture? Then she decides whether she'll work with the company. She lets the client know that she will report what she learns, not merely what the client wants to hear. "I have my values," she said.

She told me of a time when a senior executive from a multinational company insisted that she travel to meet him right away. She'd been on the road for months, only stopping at her home to pack and unpack. Nevertheless, she hopped on a plane. The senior executive represented a big client, a considerable amount of her income. "I arrived at the hotel and waited and waited," she explained, reliving the frustration. "I didn't eat because he might call. I was tired but didn't rest. I finally ate all of the peanuts in the minibar, but still no call. Five hours later, at 11 p.m. the call came. He said he'd been tied up with a client. That wasn't good enough. I told him he could have called and that I would not be meeting with him that evening. We met early the next morning. I reminded him that his company prided itself on the value of respect. I told him, 'Just because you pay me doesn't mean you own me.' He apologized sincerely. It never happened again."

Most of us aren't consultants. We can't easily pick and choose the political environments in which we work. Yet we can familiarize ourselves with the level of political pathology in our workplace and determine what that pathology means in terms of daily interactions. We can decide whether hanging on to a job that causes us to be other than ourselves really is worth it.

I was once asked to help a group of stock exchange traders reduce their level of conflict, which had reached pathological proportions. All of them were young, bright, and capable, but they despised each other and competed relentlessly. The most common form of interaction was the exchange of surface pleasantries accompanied by vicious jabs, which they'd come to call "sleazing." It got to the point where deviousness was the norm. For example, when a trader missed a meeting of an important task group due to illness, another one—who wasn't even a member of the group—attended the meeting in his place and used the opportunity to disparage his absent colleague. Games of gotcha were commonplace as each person tried to outdo the other using underhanded tactics. After identifying the primary culprits (although by this time all were guilty), I brought the traders together to discuss how to go forward. For nearly a half hour they complimented each other, denied any negative intentions, and did nothing but flatter one another; finally one member of the group interjected with evident frustration, "Who are we kidding? We despise each other most of the time." Looking directly into the eyes of each liar, she proceeded to describe each one's more recent transgressions. Then one red-faced trader pointed a finger at another, and the floodgates opened. Attacks and counterattacks were levied, but progress was made and steps agreed to, all because one person decided to do what needed to be done. She knew the possible costs, but as a street fighter she was up to the challenge.

In business, often this kind of step-up-to-the-plate, barely noticeable act of courage changes the course of events. Opposition to a popular view or behavior pattern, loyalty to a colleague under attack, leadership however unpopular in a time of crisis, firm defense of moral standards, or resolve in the face of disparagement or doubt occurs every day at some level. Whether big or small, visible or behind closed doors, most courageous acts are characterized by what psychology professor Mihaly Csikszentmihalyi describes as "flow"— a kind of mental immersion in the task at hand so strong that problems and threats are forgotten. Also, anything not directly related to that task is forced out of consciousness.[3] The goal is all-consuming and powerful in its relentlessness.

This is the kind of attitude that allowed, enabled actually, Henry B. Gonzalez to become the first Mexican American ever elected to the U.S. Congress. According to author Pete Hamill's article in Caroline Kennedy's *Profiles in Courage for Our Time*,[4] Gonzalez dedicated his life to public service. His one regret: He allowed President Lyndon Johnson to strong-arm him into a vote that opened the way for years of war in Vietnam. He vowed to never vote out of fear again. He threw himself into his work—evidenced by his small book-lined office, frugal spending, and off-the-rack clothes. His work was consuming, and he was relentless—two characteristics of flow. By 1989, despite his advanced age, he became chairman of the powerful House Banking, Finance and Urban Affairs Committee. Gonzalez demanded that the Federal Reserve Board open its proceedings to public scrutiny. He hammered away at corruption in the savings-and-loans industry, even though that meant attacking people in high places from his own political party. And he surely made enemies when he unearthed "Iraqgate"—the financial support the United States supplied to Saddam Hussein for the development of weapons. When pressed to drop the investigation for reasons of national security, Gonzalez refused.

When he finished his stint as chair (when he was forced out by ageism, some would say), Gonzalez made no attempt to make deals to keep his position. Instead, he said something few people can say with such conviction: "I have served with honor and integrity and success. I have never failed myself, and I have never failed you."

You would think that a single man from poor beginnings would have avoided altercations with bigshots who could harm his career. But Gonzalez believed that although anyone who takes a risk faces a difficult path, honesty and the courage of your convictions raises the chances of success. He said in 1994: "Once I got into politics, I learned this very early: people will respond to you if they can believe what you say. People will trust you if you keep your word. People will respect you if you respect yourself. If you lay out the problem accurately and if you propose a reasonable solution, people will give you a chance, notwithstanding your heritage or race."[5]

Gonzalez's story pertains to government and business politics. When you're on the right side, when you've looked fear in the face, when you know how politics works and know how to work with it, then little can stop you.

WHY BE COURAGEOUS?

We can all understand the importance of courage when defending one's country, but why be courageous in business? Why learn to manage politics and stick your neck out when laying low might be the easier route? If you don't have an answer to this question, then you're unlikely to be courageous.

For many people, work is a means of self-definition. "What do you do?" is usually one of the first questions we ask upon meeting someone. "I spend my days being pushed around by bullies with despicable goals" or "I do my job, keep my head down, and pray that 5 P.M. will come around quickly" would be accurate descriptions of a work life without courage. Of course, no one says things like this. But if courage is not a part of your repertoire, then it's unlikely that you're advancing good causes; in fact, you may be advancing ones that are counterproductive to your career, organization, and well-being. When people are unable to step up and stand up for themselves, others, and what they believe in because they fear they'll be in harm's way, that is exactly where they have placed themselves.

Courage also makes us more interesting to others and to ourselves. It's easy to lose sight of the goal of making ourselves interesting, especially at work. We do what we're asked, do as we're told, fly below the radar, or blend in with the scenery, essentially become boring. This may be a form of life, but it isn't living and it's far from constructive. Breathing a sigh of relief at the end of the day because it has passed without incident is enervating, not invigorating. Courage stirs the passions, gets the blood going.

Additionally, courage awakens something within, causing us to grow. Child expert Jean Piaget argued that children learn when novel events upset the normal course of things.[6] At those points, children pay more attention. Courage does this for adults partly because it is so rare, but also because it is so interesting. Its exercise opens avenues once unnoticed or closed. Ask anyone in business, as I have hundreds of times, to share with you a political experience that stands out in his or her mind. Most will tell with renewed self-satisfaction a story of how they took a risk and made a difference.

Courage is not always of the moral type. Every company needs the core competence of innovation. Yet most organizations emphasize risk aversion and exhibit a penchant for management by consensus. It takes courage to try something new because it is often misinterpreted as "bucking the system" or even disloyalty.

Organizations can benefit from the courage of their employees only if they know how to encourage and reward it. If you wonder why your company isn't more competitive, look at whether courage is drummed out of employees. Are managers worried that their subordinates might seem brighter or more technically competent than they are if subordinates are allowed to express new ideas? Does the success of subordinates reflect well on their mentors? If not, then the organization deserves to be left in the dust by competitors who have nurtured a climate of courage. Indeed, it takes courage to allow someone, especially someone younger, to seem smarter or more creative. Andrew Carnegie, the steel magnate, was not afraid to be out-smarted. On his tombstone he had engraved these words: "Here lies one who knew how to get around him men who were cleverer than himself."

Of course, courage is not a virtue that should be squandered. It invariably carries a price tag. It courts failure. Speaking up for a colleague who's been unfairly disparaged, taking a stand against a popular view or person, and refusing to take part in unethical practices can be costly. In a blame-oriented environment where finger-pointing and scapegoating are the norm, it's just plain dangerous to be fighting all of the time. Some causes are not worth that cost. Engaging in business calls for compromises. Indeed, living with other people calls for them. A marketing manager told me that each time he slips into blaming others, he pays for it. People turn away when he gets off elevators, their memories of his attacks clanging like tin cans tied to his back. Similarly, those employees who believe that their criticisms are always welcome often find themselves ostracized or even fired.

No one can, nor should anyone, be courageous all of the time, which is why courage is such an esteemed characteristic. Going down to one defeat after another is not the hallmark of courage; it is an invitation to early and wasteful demise. As Yale law professor Stephen L. Carter writes in his book, *Integrity*, "True, all of us should be steadfast and uncompromising about *something*, but only the fanatic is steadfast and uncompromising about *everything*."[7]

If you're going to be courageous, it pays to possess the political know-how regarding when, where, and how to proceed. This knowledge keeps political suicide at bay.

WHAT POLITICAL COURAGE REQUIRES

Can you tell me, Socrates, whether virtue is taught? Or is it not taught, but acquired by practice? Or is it neither acquired by practice or learnt, but does it arise in people by nature or in some other way?

This is Meno's first question to Socrates in Plato's *Meno*. The answer to this question vexed philosophers for centuries to come. According to Aristotle, courage is a facing of danger in the right way and at the right time. It is not something forced so much as a desire to be noble, to avoid reproach or disgrace. Courage, from this perspective, is what a person's honor and reputation require and is therefore at least partially learned. It also comes largely from within, Aristotle would argue were he here today, not from demands imposed solely by the situation or by others.

Courage is made possible when something an individual stands for, believes in, holds dear, or intensely desires is significantly threatened. It rarely comes from fear of what others might say. In fact, such fear tends to give rise to caution. President Harry Truman once said, "I wonder how far Moses would have gone if he'd taken a poll in Egypt."[8] A prerequisite to courage, then, is a deep sense of what matters most. Is a pat on the back more important than self-satisfaction? Is a job tomorrow, no matter the cost, more important than defense of a friend? Is pleasing the big shots or all of those who work for you a higher priority than heeding the call of your own conscience? If you don't have answers to such questions, courage is unlikely, if not impossible, because it cannot exist without reflection on priorities. All of the people I've interviewed who have demonstrated courage described in one way or another the existence of a personal sense of "center"—a knowledge of self in terms of priorities of purpose, the bedrock of considered action.

These comments from the CFO of a leading clothing manufacturer demonstrate the kind of thinking that creates a sense of center requisite to courage.

> I have had two "moments of truth" in my career. The first occurred at the bank where I had gradually begun to feel that the professional environment and my personal values were incompatible. I did not know what to do about this, since I had no other job lined up, and the bank was

paying for my master's degree. However, one day I was speaking with my boss, the CFO, who commented that we needed to reduce some operational staff in the foreign exchange area. I informed him that we were already understaffed and that this specific area had been targeted for strategic growth. He thought for a minute, and then said, "Well, why don't we just get rid of some computers or desks?" I am sure he did not realize what he'd just said, but to me it was one of those eye-opening, jaw-dropping moments. The organization considered people, desks, and computers as interchangeable. They simply were disposable assets to be used and discarded at the whim of management. I left that day knowing positively that I would never work in that type of environment again. I sat down and summarized the five most critical work considerations in any future endeavor I would undertake. My commitment was:

- To do meaningful work that I love
- To be proud of the company for which I worked, and proud to tell people that I worked there
- To work in a company where at least half the employees are women, and where women fill at least half of the senior management positions
- To work in a company that had a higher mission and that produced a product that was fun, valuable, or beneficial to society
- To work in a company where my personal values and the values of the company were the same

The very next day after sitting down and writing this list, I learned that a company I'd longed to work for was looking for a CFO. I contacted them, interviewed, and started a few weeks later. It was ironic because if need be I was thoroughly reconciled to working at a garden nursery for minimum wage. That would have fit all of my goals. However, I ended up in a wonderful company making significantly more money than I was making in banking.

Political courage rests on a foundation of established priorities like these. In this example, the new company served the CEO's personal philosophy. Other courage-evoking philosophies are societal, organizational, or group oriented. They guide choices and often elicit small courageous moments that, although less visible than are public, celebrated acts of courage, often make a significant impact.

One manager I interviewed divides battles into three types in order to guide his decisions:

1. Those I don't feel strongly about, but for which I have a slight preference for a particular outcome. In these cases, I use the battle as a negotiating point—something I am willing to give up in trade.
2. Those I do feel strongly about, but are not values related or moral issues. Here I use all data available to make my point, but I remain willing to be persuaded.
3. Values conflicts or moral issues. This is where I put my spear in the sand and fight.

Having even a basic set of categories like these can help you determine whether courage is required.

POLITICAL ACUMEN

Knowing why courage matters and creating your personal philosophy is a strong start on the road to becoming courageous at work. Without political acumen, however, even the best intentions go awry. For example, in most instances where courage is a choice, the decision to be courageous should be prefaced by these questions: Is this the right time? Do I have the needed support? Is my track record sufficiently developed? If I go to the mat on this, what is the upside and what is the downside? Who stands to lose? Who will gain? Will the results be worth the damage? Am I up to the challenge?

These are not questions meant to bring about retreat. They are means to help you size up the situation. When emotions run high on an issue, it's difficult to step back to assess potential gains and losses, but that's exactly what needs to be done. With the exception of the military courage needed to storm a beach or take a hill, which calls for putting reason aside, most acts of courage ultimately are driven by emotion. This is especially the case at work. Courage at work is usually about standing up to a corrupt or dangerous coalition or powerful individual. It is about standing one's ground when others run or slip away, dodge responsibility, or refuse to take what they know to be the more admirable route. At work, you must consider whether bringing others to their senses is worth the battle and whether now is the time to do so.

I remember observing a senior manager take the side of a friend at a meeting that was called to deny this friend promotion. Some behind-the-scenes meetings evidently had taken place beforehand; only weeks before his friend seemed a shoo-in, but now both his work and his potential were the target of brutal attacks. The senior manager possessed considerable power, but he faced power in numbers at this meeting. He confidently asserted that his friend was and always had been slated for promotion. I sat in on the meeting as he presented a strong case. There was no doubt that he was in the right, that his friend was being treated unfairly. The senior manager fought relentlessly for a time, until he fully noticed the intensity of the opposition, at which point he began to lessen his protests. The vote was taken. He and one other raised their hands in support of his friend, but no one else did. Nothing more was said. I admit that my respect waned a bit for this senior manager. I'd seen him take on powerful adversaries. He was a force to be reckoned with. Yet this time he declined to finish his fight. When the meeting was over, he left without a word. He'd lost—something that had rarely happened to him before. But less than two weeks later, he did something not often done in business: He hired to his division the man who had not been promoted, giving him a high-level position without asking anyone who'd attended the meeting for his or her blessing. Instead, he got the go-ahead from a vice president who'd long respected him and who owed him support. His new hire proved to be one of the most impressive on his staff, both loyal and competent; he'd been snatched from the jaws of defeat by the senior manager who'd clearly known when to sidestep a direct battle to win on the sidelines. The people who'd voted against the new hire might have complained or attempted to undermine the senior manager, but they did not do so. Some even implied they'd been supportive all along, that they knew the rejected candidate would land on his feet. There are no limits to which some people will go to cover their tracks. The senior manager's strategy had been more of a sidestep than the frontal offense characteristic of most acts of courage, but it had been courageous nonetheless.

Courage does not take only one form, nor is it always characterized by a single bold act. In fact, it often takes place over time. As this story demonstrates, occasionally determination must be rerouted toward a more propitious goal. Had the senior manager allowed anger to take hold, had he belittled his peers by reminding them of promises they'd made to the candidate, had he protested being left out of the loop or promised revenge, it would have been to no avail. He might have had his say, but the cost would have been dear. There are times when the cost is worth it, but if the die is cast against you and another route might provide reasonable results, then that's the course to take. Hiring the man spoke volumes in terms of power. It said: You can try to block me in one way, but I'll find another. People who can find creative solutions like this are a force to be reckoned with, and most people will not try to undermine them a second time.

What enabled this senior manager to make such a decision? Most people would have left the room knowing they'd fought a good fight, even if it hadn't been their best one. They would have rationalized that they'd done what they could, but few would have the chutzpah to do what this man did. He knew there were risks to his action, but he felt comfortable with them. Clearly he had conviction and an admirable sense of justice. But sometimes people with these characteristics swallow hard and accept a defeat in order to prevent a political disaster for themselves. What was different here? This question brings us to other conditions and skills needed to be courageous.

TRACK RECORD

A good track record is an important prerequisite to acting courageously at work. Without a solid track record, actions like the one taken by this senior manager could lead to political suicide. He not only opposed the majority, but he also came up with his own way of doing what he considered right. This action made some feel blindsided. But anyone who protested would have had to go up against a man of unquestioned competence and political acumen. Rather than the act of a petulant underling, the action was that of a determined colleague who could, if need be, turn into a formidable adversary. The senior manager told me he knew that no rational person would challenge him alone, and he also knew that they were not all of one mind. Their collusion had been born of pressure by a few. Those who'd gone along for the sake of harmony now saw that their actions had been in support of a paper tiger; the real tiger had won the day. In one action the senior manager had demonstrated not only that he still had power, but also that he knew how to use it in the face of majority opposition.

A track-record prerequisite doesn't mean that young people can't be courageous. They do need to have some successes behind them if they want to make a truly bold move. Knowing the limits of your record is key. I worked with a small company whose CEO had not outlined a succession plan. His young, highly competent, but sometimes politically inexperienced executives wanted job security. They wanted him to decide who would run the company if something were to happen to him. He was getting older, they told him. He respected each of them, but he was angered by what he saw as their temerity. For weeks he froze them out, thinking they'd gone too far with what they saw as their rights. More important, they'd approached the issue too directly and too rapidly for people so young and inexperienced. They overestimated their ability to deal with a very delicate situation. What they saw as courageous was politically unwise. They overestimated how far his respect for their competence would support them, and it took a long time for the wounds to heal. This kind of overestimation can lead to political suicide.

Many young people do succeed in influencing those with seniority. "I have a thought you might want to consider," "Can I play the devil's advocate here for a moment? I did some background study for this meeting and have a point to make before you decide how to proceed," or "I don't have the experience of others here, but there's one thing we may have neglected to fully consider" are ways to introduce a challenge or to question someone in higher authority. "This may be a stupid idea" is not a good thing to say. It diminishes credibility. Listeners wonder why someone would bother to say something they believe might be stupid, let alone apologize in advance. We've already discussed the dangers of ill-considered apologies. Considerate acknowledgment of power imbalances, however, invite those who might otherwise view a junior person's challenge as impertinence to see it as a well-meaning attempt to contribute. If you make the comments worth their time, senior people will listen.

A manager turned business consultant told me that she has always been an advocate of her values, even when she was young. "Your values determine whether you'll challenge someone. As a young accountant of twenty-two, I found a business expense in the records that was questionable. It was a Christmas Day luncheon for twelve people—guests of the company president. I told my boss that I couldn't possibly sign off on the request. If it was really a business expense, he could sign. Otherwise it would have to be rejected. He attempted to convince me to sign, but I continued to refuse. If he wanted it signed, I repeated, he could sign it himself. Instead, I found myself invited to the president's office. I explained my position—told him that if he could assure me that the luncheon was indeed a legitimate business gathering that I would sign, but only under those conditions. 'Perhaps it was a business luncheon,' I offered. 'Perhaps some people do business on Christmas.' The president, to his credit, said, 'It was not a business luncheon. You were the only one to object to it. We all learn. Thank you.'"

I asked if there'd been any fallout, any revenge served to her cold. She assured me that nothing like that had happened. In fact, she gained the president's respect; he knew not to toy with her again. "I kept it very confidential," she told me. "It was between me and my mirror. They knew that and respected it."

TIMING

Archbishop Desmond Tutu captured the importance of timing for courageous leaders when he described good leaders as having intuition, defined as "the capacity to read the signs of the times, and to have this uncanny sixth sense of knowing when to go for it." He said: "The real leader knows too when to make concessions, when to compromise, when to employ the art of losing the battle in order to win the war. Some leaders make a virtue of being hardliners. You might win, and then one day comes the shattering almost ignominious loss."[9]

Patience is indeed a virtue, all the more so when much is at stake or when emotions are running high. The people I've interviewed about their acts of political courage have described themselves as risk takers, especially when someone has exceeded their threshold of tolerance, but they are not foolhardy. They assess situations quickly when need be, but not recklessly. If they sense that the emotional climate is not right for a frontal assault or that past history makes a particular move likely to incur wrath, they pause, reflect, and consider an alternative route or a delay. They are not indecisive

---

POLITICAL ADVANTAGE #12

Politically courageous people know one very important fact of life: that achieving a goal is often not as important as the way it's achieved. They realize that there's truth in the adage that winning a battle is not always the way to win a war.

---

so much as observant, not fearful so much as reflective. They know when they must act, but they wait until the timing is propitious.

Claudia Kennedy, the first female three-star U.S. Army general, wrote in her book *Generally Speaking,* "I firmly believe a person's life involves much more than achieving distant career goals."[10] She describes all leaders, including herself, as "works in progress" that continue to develop every day. Politically courageous people like Claudia Kennedy focus on the here and now, judge it for what it is, and deal with challenges, knowing that each one must be taken in its course and measured against personal standards. They know that some things are best dealt with later when conditions are more conducive. Usually the wait is not as long as it is difficult.

SIGNIFICANCE OF THE ISSUE

I worked for several years with Betty Friedan, one of America's leading figures in the modern women's movement and author of the seminal work, *The Feminine Mystique.* Some days Betty was so focused, so impatient with distraction that she angered people. Yet this was one reason why she also was so successful in bringing women out of their 1960s kitchens onto the streets to insist on their rights. For example, more than once she expressed annoyance with people who publicly asked her where she stood on pornography. "It's not the issue," she'd nearly shout. She would not be distracted or be quoted if there was any chance that attention would be pulled away from the view she was advancing. When we lectured together at the University of Southern California's Marshall School, although we'd laughed, argued, planned, and even shopped together, I knew I was standing beside someone who'd made history. She'd done so in part by knowing the difference between issues that divide and ones that bring solidarity. She never cowered from a fight, whether in front of the Oak Bar in the New York Plaza Hotel in the 1960s, when they wouldn't let her in because she was a woman, or with her peers in the National Organization of Women. Unlike most people I've met, she knew which fights to fight. She talked for hours with friends, debated, considered, and even one time, at a Dublin women's conference, telephoned my hotel room before 5 A.M. to invite me for a thought walk. I went, and, as usual, we covered a lot of territory, not only in miles, but also in conversation, intensely debating issues she'd be speaking about later in the day. She always listened to others, after which she'd decide her own view; then, damn the torpedoes, she'd stay on course.

Effectively courageous people don't allow themselves to be distracted by minor issues. They know that focusing too much time on trivial matters threatens their enduring focus. Each of us must recognize this truth if our actions are to matter, if we're to leave a legacy marked by consistent strides toward a worthwhile goal. There may be people who disagree with Betty Friedan, and some days even we had our moments, but she is admired by millions and will be respected by history because she stood for something very significant and never wavered.

EXTENT OF THE RISK

There are four questions to ask before taking a significant risk at work on an issue. The answers shouldn't necessarily deter us from courage, but they should make us wiser going forward:

1. Who will likely win?
2. Who will likely lose?
3. Who will try to get you later if you win?
4. Who's out to get you already?

I remember a discussion about revenge that took place in one of my executive MBA classes. One female student said, "I always marvel at how men are able to fight viciously and then go out and play golf." A few people replied with the view that men are less likely to hold grudges, but one very perceptive, and that day very forthcoming, student said, "That's what a lot of women think. But we guys know that while we're playing golf we're thinking 'I'll get that so-and-so someday.'" That's one thing politicians know: Revenge is not always immediate. You have to remain alert. Always assess the revenge landscape before taking a political risk. Make sure your cannons are in place and that your future nemesis doesn't have nuclear weapons. Courage may require bravery, but not the blind kind. If you don't have the skill or stamina to go the distance, then perhaps this isn't the best moment to be courageous. Gather support, assess the potential damage, and, when possible, identify a way to make your point without rubbing someone's nose in the dirt. Otherwise, prepare yourself for years of watching your back.

A New York public relations director for a leading insurance company told me of a peer who thought the human resources department was the place to bring complaints. He naively went to see an HR representative without giving a thought to the company's political climate. He spilled the beans, named names, pointed fingers, and drew blood. He thought he was being courageous. "He didn't last long after that," the HR director said. "He began receiving memos about the quality of his work, he was assigned to go-nowhere projects, and he was left out of anything important.

You have to know the kind of place you're working in before taking career risks. Many countries have suffered in wars because they didn't understand the terrain on which they were fighting, to say nothing of the enemy and the lengths to which they'd go to win. If you don't know the terrain and the enemy and the guises they can take, then the risk is likely too great.

All this preparation for courageous acts may seem a tall order. And, indeed, there are times when it's impossible. But courage at work is a choice and one not to be taken lightly. Don't squander your talent through political recklessness at work. Make sure that the time is right for your acts of courage, the issues are worthy of the risk, your ducks are lined up, and your win and no-win options are defined. If you are up to the challenge in terms of strategy and determined, then go for it. Few things make the blood run and heart pound like courage in the service of doing the right thing, and few things make such an appreciable, memorable difference.

CHAPTER EIGHT

POSITIVE POLITICS

To educate a man in mind and not in morals is to educate a
menace to society.

—Theodore Roosevelt

A NUMBER OF business schools are hard at work attempting to
develop ethics courses. The moral decline of business weighs
on the minds of those who were appalled by business ethics fiascos
of Enron, Tyco, and Global Crossing, among others. Yet even the
most erudite among us are at somewhat of a loss when establishing
ethics guidelines for business. After all, business is widely considered to be first and foremost about profit. Unlike governments,
which are supposed to work for the interests of the public, most
businesses operate in the interests of shareholders or owners. Without any widely accepted standards of political ethics or virtue, businesses are left to their own devices. Most give mere lip service to
political virtues—standards by which behaviors should be guided to
avoid political pathology—and few overtly reward those who are
guided by such virtues.

When I use the word "virtue," I'm referring to its use as a means
of becoming a good person. For the ancient Greeks, medieval the-
ologians, and many contemporary philosophers, the cultivation of
virtue makes people happy, wise, courageous, and competent.

What results is a good person, a responsible citizen and parent, a trusted leader, and at the extreme, a saint.[1] To run well and to establish a common good, society depends on the existence of virtuous people.

This is all very highbrow, but a look at what exists today with regard to virtue might convince even the most entrenched skeptics that a return to consideration of virtue—ethics, if you will—is long overdue. We live in an age of moral relativism. Ideas of right and wrong are a matter of opinion. There are few, if any, ground rules. Some philosophers, such as James Q. Wilson, Ronald Reagan Professor of Public Policy at Pepperdine University, recommend talking about four virtues as old as Aristotle: prudence, justice, fortitude, and temperance. In his book *The Moral Sense*, Wilson adds a fifth: compassion.[2] Prudence is not caution, so much as the practical wisdom involved in recognizing and making the right choices in specific situations. It is the "master virtue" that makes all others possible. Justice, according to the Greeks, includes fairness, honesty, and keeping promises. Fortitude is courage in pursuit of the right path, and temperance is self-discipline. Compassion is an extension of concern to strangers that we more readily extend to family members and friends. A good person, it could be argued then, is one who achieves a balance of these virtues exemplified in consistent good acts.

How is this balance achieved? Aristotle argued that practice is the key. Role models are the means by which children learn to be virtuous. But today available role models must be an addition to introspection. Should temperance be given greater weight than prudence? Rather than throw up our hands and admit defeat, we should—in fact, we must—engage in a discussion at least with ourselves about the kinds of people we want to be and, in terms of politics, just how far we're willing to veer from the "virtuous" end of the spectrum.

It's important to ask whether there is a point at which politics run amok begins to devour who we are and the economic and social fabrics of business. If we are unable to come to some understanding of when politics is unacceptable, then unethical practices will continue to cannibalize institutions and individuals. Companies run by people oblivious of politics or unwilling to manage it eventually eat away at the very structures that afforded their development. Every organization and, indeed, every worker should assess whether and how they have crossed the line into destructive politics. That way, when we find ourselves at political choice points, we won't be unprepared or forced to react in kind to devious or despicable acts.

By developing a political compass, you also come to understand the full range of good and bad. You will come to understand not only what you want to be like but also what you reject. In so doing, you also will get a glimpse into the world of con men, scam artists, and others who take advantage of a trusting nature. Knowing how the other side thinks and what aspects of that thinking you reject is always valuable. When you set boundaries regarding what you won't do, a bad apple won't be able to spoil your barrel—at least not with you in it. You can leave the barrel or help rejuvenate it. You can pick a better apple and refuse to define your actions as good or bad based on a rotten taste.

DEVELOPING YOUR POLITICAL COMPASS

The first step in becoming aware of your political limits is to objectively reflect on how you tend to act. Doing this can be tricky. Because we bring along our sense-making habits and desires whenever we interpret events of any kind, we thereby influence what we observe. If we want to be ethical, we lean toward seeing ourselves as such. A man who uses biting sarcasm to berate someone from another political party may consider the same kind of attack on him to be uncivilized. Similarly, we tend to forgive ourselves and those we respect or befriend more than we forgive others. This tendency gets in the way of honest self-assessment. For example, we give what psychologists call "idiosyncracy credits" to some people.[3] These are like social credits that allow the beneficiary to tell bad jokes, talk too much, be rude and get away with it—in other words, to be excused from social gaffes. "Oh, you know Sara. She's always like that. She doesn't mean any harm" is the kind of thing that might be said to excuse what would otherwise be seen as bad form, crass behavior, or incivility. We give license to those we like or admire.

Often we extend the same courtesy to ourselves. We blame our questionable behavior on circumstances or other people. We do this especially if we operate more from an external control orientation than from an internal one.[4] *Externals* blame conditions, rather than themselves, for bad outcomes. "She made me do it," "That stop sign was not visible," "People were pressuring me, so what could I do?" are the kinds of things externals say to explain or excuse their actions. *Internals,* by contrast, see themselves as the causal agents of what happens to them and what they do in response. "I did it and there's really no good excuse," "I should have seen that coming," "If I'd done my homework, none of this would have happened" are examples of how internals talk.[5]

It isn't good to be too external or too internal in your orientation. If you always blame others, you will never examine yourself. If you always blame yourself, you will never examine how conditions might be affecting you and how they might be changed to bring about better, more admirable responses from you. It's better to have a balance of internal and external orientation in your assessment of factors influencing the things you do. That's the first step in developing what I call a *personal political compass,* which is a method for assessing direction in terms of ethics. Your political compass asks: Am I getting close to crossing the line into the gray area of ethics? Am I heading directly into the danger zone?

Would you use a bridge without guide rails to cross over sea and

---

POLITICAL ADVANTAGE #13

Without a political compass, it's a lot easier to slip into political ways of acting and being that go against what you truly believe in.

---

rocks hundreds of feet below? Probably not. Then why would you enter politically precarious situations without some guide to get you safely through without doing damage to who you are and what you believe in?

Now that we've established why we all need a political compass, the next step is to go about developing one. When I was an undergraduate, a wise professor told my class that people remember 20 percent of what you tell them and 80 percent of what they do. That's why the next part of this chapter is about "doing." It consists of several hypothetical situations you can use to assess the current state of your political compass and to work at developing it to be more useful and comfortable for you. While putting yourself in a hypothetical situation isn't exactly "doing" in the sense of true action, it's a better learning tool than pure lecture. Rather than go on about what an individual political compass should look like, let's work through some situations. You'll find that each of them could easily lead to negative political reactions, but your focus should be on how to use positive political responses instead.

As you'll see in some of the suggested responses, positive politics is not all sweetness and light. It's constructive in the sense that it involves taking the high road and sparing relationships from harm whenever possible. There are times even in positive political responses when conflict is unavoidable and when confronting someone is necessary. Just don't let the situation deteriorate into name-calling, backstabbing, and viciousness. Positive politics repairs or reconfigures a situation in order to produce a *reasonably* positive result. I use the word "reasonably" because situations at work can become very emotional and tempers can take over. We can't always be at our best, though we should strive for it. Even Dorothy in the *Wizard of Oz* was reduced to slapping the lion to get him to calm down. That wasn't one of her better actions, but her stress level was high. She could have done worse. We can understand her action, given that she was a child dealing with an out-of-control witch. In situations of high stress, a political compass comes in handy. Had Dorothy had one, the lion might have gotten off a bit easier.

As a first step in developing your political compass, think about how you'd handle the following situations, keeping in mind the virtues of prudence, justice, fortitude, temperance, and compassion. People often do nothing in response to ethical dilemmas because they haven't developed a repertoire of responses. Practicing with the following scenarios is a start, although they're generic and so may not reflect the climate in which you work. Feel free to modify the suggested solutions so long as you remember that each is intended to avoid negative politics.

SITUATION 1
Credit Snatching

You just watched your boss present one of your ideas as if it were her own. What do you do?

First you need to consider whether this is the first time your boss has done this. If it is, then there's a chance that this was an oversight on her part. It's important to separate *offense* from *insult* at work. We all offend each other now and then. Accidental offenses call for a gentle reminder or even overlooking the offense. But if you tell your boss she's offended you and she does it again, then you've been insulted. This requires a stronger response. If your boss often steals your ideas, you need to have a heart-to-heart with her. Find out what she expects of you. If she defines your job simply as making her look good and you can't live with that, get out your résumé. If she seems determined to ensure that your contributions are noticed, then consider telling her that you were a bit uncomfortable when she introduced the idea as if it were her own. See what she has to say. Remember that taking this candid route is risky; your boss could get offended. Be sure you have other options, that you haven't put all your eggs in this basket. If you have other options, you'll be approaching this situation from a position of strength, and that tends to be persuasive.

SITUATION 2
"It'll Ruin Your Career" Threat

You've been told that standing up to one of your peers, who on several occasions has attempted to publicly demean you, could ruin your career. Apparently he knows a lot of people in high places, and he's vindictive. The latest incident occurred after you misstated the delivery date for your team's project. Your detractor smirked and shook his head as if to say "There you go again making mistakes." He then said, "Why do you bother coming if you can't adequately prepare? You don't even know when we're supposed to have this project completed. You shouldn't be in a leadership role on this project if you don't know what's going on."

First, it's good to remember that anyone who acts like this has a problem that's likely unrelated to you. Nevertheless, this man has put you on the spot. Consider this as well: He has publicly attacked you and even questioned your leadership. Can you just let that pass? If he does have power, especially the power to "ruin your career," then you'll need to respond intelligently. Remember that anyone who is allowed to continue to treat you this way may ruin your job, but no one can ruin your career except you. Certain people can make it difficult to work at a number of places, but it's unlikely that one person can totally ruin you. Besides, he has targeted you, and once you're a target—a public one at that—worrying about being one later is missing the point. You need to deal with the here-and-now.

If you don't want to respond in an intensely negative way, consider saying: "If leadership depends on never making a misstatement, then I'd say no one will be spared." You could add, "and that includes you" if you're feeling spirited. He may respond with "At least I know when the project is due." Rather than defend yourself, as people will likely expect, you might take a diversion: "Is there something bothering you that we should get out in the open?" Say this calmly. If he gets angry, try taking the high road with "All of us here are working toward the same goal, so why don't we focus on getting this project done well? That seems the path of greater benefit."

If your detractor continues to berate you, it may be time to give him a little of his own medicine. Before going to battle in front of everyone, suggest a break. Take him aside, and try to work things out privately. You could say, "We can't spare any more time in there with us barking at each other, so if you have anything else you want to say to me of a derogatory nature, say it now." Let him vent. Then consider saying "Fine. I've heard you out. I'll think about all of this. Now, let's go back in there and work together. I don't want you as an enemy, but believe me, you don't want me as one either." If he starts to demean you again after the meeting gets under way, remind him of your agreement. Let the others hear you. "At the break we decided to put our differences aside so the team can function. I suggest we continue to do that." If you say this with confidence and a calm expression, then he will be hard-pressed to attack again as he'll appear to be violating an agreement and also putting his petty hatred ahead of the needs of the team.

SITUATION 3
Targeting

You know that your boss, whom you don't really respect, is out to get someone you do respect. Should you let that person know?

In this test of ethics, the virtues of compassion and prudence are at odds. The prudent or practical thing to do might be to stay out of this situation. If you inform your boss's target, he might confront your boss with the information and reveal his source. Ultimately, most people would consider the nature of their relationship with the targeted person. If you're an ethical purist, you might feel inclined or compelled to share what you know no matter the extent of the relationship. Or you might confront your boss directly. This kind of directness, however, is rarely the most politically productive. It airs the problem if your boss is willing to own up to it, but it might cause him to lose face, perhaps unnecessarily. In such politically delicate situations, the first step is to ask yourself a question: Do I have enough data to be sure of my conclusion? This isn't a stalling tactic; it's an important step. You don't want to assume. Get some background information. Find out what the other person might have done to anger or threaten your boss. Perhaps ask someone you trust about your suspicions. Has something like this happened before? Make your inquiry informal, and don't provide too much information. Perhaps mention that you noticed the assumed target seems to be criticized quite often. You also could go directly to the boss and ask whether the person has done something that's put him in the doghouse with people here. Find out what the targeted person did to deserve this kind of "special attention." Once you've collected these data, you can determine whether to give the targeted person a heads-up or to go to her defense without her knowledge. This is a tough decision and there's a downside, especially if your boss believes you're uncomfortable with his actions. There are no right answers to this scenario, only better and worse ones. But whatever you do, don't do it without checking your assumptions and determining how much responsibility to take. Should you protect the targeted person, or should you inform her and then let her take things from there? If this kind of targeting happens regularly in your company or division, you might want to find somewhere else to work. No one is safe in this kind of environment.

SITUATION 4
Scapegoating

You receive an e-mail copied to all project team members describing your work as "below expectations." You realize that you're taking the fall for mistakes made by people in the project's inner circle—a dangerous clique whose members likely colluded in the creation of this e-mail.

A natural inclination here would be to defend yourself by deflecting blame. But "I wasn't the one who did this. You're to blame" isn't a positive approach. Remember, a lot of people are probably laying low, hoping the blame won't be placed on them, so they aren't about to run to your aid without good reason. Yet "Eating these kinds of things by being passive isn't the best approach," one New York–based senior manager advises. "They'll just keep doing it to you. Besides, it's one thing to be hoisted for what you did and entirely another thing to be hoisted for something you *didn't* do."

One way to handle this situation is by admitting (in an e-mail or in the next meeting) only to a small error or a vaguely related one. In other words, let the team know that while you're not claiming perfection, you won't own up to mistakes you didn't make. You might say, "You know I'm the first to point out my mistakes. For example, I was wrong about X, but taking the fall for Y is something I'm not about to do." No need to place the blame elsewhere. First, get it off your back. "I don't point fingers and appreciate when they aren't pointed at me. I suggest we move on and get the project done." Should someone challenge you, avoid retaliation. Instead, focus on the project goals: "The project is our highest priority." You could say, "I could list other people's errors, as I'm sure anyone in this room could do, but that won't get us where we want to be. It'll sure give our competition a welcome time advantage." In situations where the person who disparaged you is a maneuverer and isn't likely to back off easily, you might say, "Do we really want to go down that path? I have a long memory. If you want to go tit-for-tat and see who comes out the winner, then fine. But if you want to get this project done, let's end the blame game and move on." This latter approach is an example of brinksmanship. It goes to the edge of civility, forcing the other party's hand. Before you go this route, be sure you're right and have support. There's always the hypothetical

"What if you were right?" approach: "I can see why my name would come up in the search for blame. And I'm not the easiest person to get along with at times. But ask yourself this: Would I actually do what would surely make me an enemy, and rightly so, of this entire team? I may be a bit abrasive at times, but I'm not stupid."

If this is a tough group, you may need to offer to name names to show that you aren't about to let them walk all over you. Start by saying "I didn't last this long here by taking shots I didn't deserve, and I'm not about to start doing so now." Then turn to someone respected who is likely to sympathize. "Sam, you wouldn't swallow blame you didn't deserve. Neither will I." If you say this with conviction and avoid threatening anyone, Sam or another team member might step forward with a proposed solution that removes the blame from you.

Keep in mind, though, that you probably can live with this kind of situation now and then, but it can be very stressful as a steady diet. If such situations are common where you work, you'd better get good at handling them. Watch what the politically astute say and do. There are likely a few lessons awaiting you.

SITUATION 5
Patronizing

Someone senior to you by one level dismisses what you say at meetings with a sneer and a laugh. She verbally belittles your contributions and tries, with some success, to bring others into the game.

The natural inclination here is to make feeble attempts at protective humor or to be silent until you finally blow up or leave in anger or distress. Neither of these approaches is constructive. If someone is bullying you in this way, you need to bring it to a halt. If you've let the situation go on for some time, changing the behavior won't be easy. However, you still can make some positive moves. Consider using one of the following responses.

"Mary, you've had a lot of fun at my expense, but it's likely
becoming a bit boring to others. It certainly has with me."
"I wonder sometimes, Mary, whether you belittle people because you're not happy working on this team."
"How is it, Mary, that I've become your favored target?"

You also can do what a senior television news journalist told
me she'd do. First she'd try to remedy the situation with sweetness
and optimism. If it were to go on, she'd get support, then go into
the offender's office and say, "If you don't want me for an enemy,
and no one here does, you'd better bring a halt to these attacks
right now." This approach is called "firing a shot across their bow."
Some shots are subtler than this, but if someone has been patronizing you for a long time, subtlety isn't likely to work. Viciousness
isn't necessary, and in some cultures it's a sign of failure, but, at
times, directness is just what's needed. You need support to take
this approach, so be sure to line up supporters. Get key people on
your side first; then let the insulting person know you mean business. That's still positive politics. You haven't stabbed anyone in
the back; you've let the person know that it's wise not to mess with
you. There's a difference.

Those who derive joy from bringing sadness to others only respect power and often fall away when they see that things are not
going their way. Trust your gut when someone appears to be self-
serving in advancing his own agenda. Know the types who draw
blood for their own amusement and target others to create a distraction from their own mischief. Deal with them early and
swiftly, as poison has few antidotes once it has spread throughout
a group.

This is politics in the ethical gray area, but when you're dealing
with someone who'll stoop to any level to get what she wants, you
aren't playing a child's game. You needn't be as vicious as the other
person, but you should be quick on your feet and clever.

SITUATION 6
The Double Bind

You can't seem to please your boss. You did what he said would get you a promotion, but now he tells you that kind of work is no longer valued. He says he sympathizes with you but he's powerless. The people upstairs call the shots.

This is sometimes referred to as slippery criteria. Up until a point in time certain types of achievement matter, and then, just when you've accomplished those, another one becomes more important. Sometimes it's a game, a way of getting work out of people without rewarding them. The first step here is to lessen your dependency on your boss. Take the control over your future out of the hands of someone who can't be clear and consistent. Talk to those who've thrived in the system and who know what gets rewarded. Learn what to do to boost your chances of being rewarded with a plum assignment, a pat on the back, or a promotion. Don't get mad or even; just get away from this boss. Don't waste another moment chasing after the next target he or she describes. It's likely another dud. Once you know what really counts, work on that. You don't need to alienate your supervisor by expressing anger, just don't take on time-consuming jobs at this boss's instruction if you can avoid doing so. Start looking for another boss, or else find someone who can exert some pressure on yours to give you a fair chance. Do these things quietly. Don't telegraph your efforts, or you may walk into work one day to discover your messages have been intercepted.

If you don't like any of these approaches, you can talk directly to your boss. In fact, you can do that first. See how it goes. Tell him you've read a book that describes the kind of constant changes in goals that you've endured. Consider telling him, if it's true, that you've gotten some advice from people who've been around the company for some time and they've advised you to find out exactly what you need to do to move up. Unless he responds with adequate assurance and clarity regarding how you can achieve a promotion, it's best to move on.

SITUATION 7
Lording

You work for someone who makes everything a power issue. Any requests you make are subject to what she calls "evaluation." What she means is you're not going to get what you want unless you demonstrate loyalty, even on simple requests.

Some people are obsessed with power. When they have little of it but like to throw what they do have in your face, it's called "lording." Lorders allocate funds and equipment as favors while making those whom they dislike or distrust wait longer for something as mundane as a wastepaper basket. These kinds of people can really get to you if you let them. But you can't let them. Doing so raises their power. Don't get mad, don't get even, just find another source for what you need. Buy your own wastebasket. Save your energy for the bigger battles. Look around for projects with budgets that might afford you autonomy to purchase what you want. Decide what really matters. Don't have a heart attack over someone's petty possessive tactics. When people wield power in this way, it's a sign of weakness, not strength. Stop caring about what the person provides. When offered something, you might want to decline graciously. Saying "Thanks, but I don't really need that right now" tells the lorder that you don't need him. Nothing bothers a lorder more than that. At some point you may want to accept an offer, but don't return to dependence—not ever.

SITUATION 8
Embedded Spies

A colleague invited you to lunch and spent the whole time pumping you for information.

POLITICAL ADVANTAGE #14

One thing to remember about business: Any question that
seems too personal probably is.

Embedded spies are in cahoots with someone. They invite you to
lunch to pick your brain and then convey anything they learn, and
some things they've made up, to someone from whom they'll derive a
favor. Anyone who takes an inordinate interest in what you think
about delicate issues is not to be trusted. Rather than say nothing
when someone pokes around for information, say little of value. Talk
around the issue. Discuss what you've heard but not what you think.
Be careful to differentiate between the two. Ask the spy what he or she
thinks. Don't slip into reciprocating with information that can be
turned against you. If the person seems forthcoming, he or she may be
using a technique social scientists call "apparent self-disclosure." This
involves acting as if you're providing a lot of information so that the
other person will feel obligated to reciprocate. I worked with a woman
who did this very well. She would close the door of her office and
whisper to give you the impression that she was telling you something
very private and important. In this way she elicited information from
people who wouldn't have provided it had they not felt a need to reciprocate. Spies are tricky. Don't be paranoid that they're lurking
around every corner, but do be cautious. If you think you're being
pumped for information, you probably are. Be pleasant, but don't
stick around long. Isn't there somewhere else you should be?

SITUATION 9
Gossiping

You confided in someone you thought was trustworthy
about a problem in your personal life, and now you find
that he used that information to raise his value with a more
senior person. The impression he created is that you're distracted.

Gossip exists all around the world. In some places it's practically a national pastime. Anthropologists tell us that we gossip to position ourselves above others. Gossip can be used in this way at work, but it also can be used to bring people down from an enviable position. If you've been stung, take it as a lesson. You could go to the person who used you and protest, but what would that get you? It's usually better to go home and think about a strategy. How can you deal with this situation without giving the offending person more power? Often the best strategy is to let some time pass. Put things into perspective. We all get talked about. Unless it was particularly virulent gossip, you could take it as an indication of jealousy, which often is at the root of gossip. Even if you don't see this as a legitimate excuse, take the high road in your response. If you approach the gossiper, do it when the two of you are alone. You might say, "What prompted you to share what I told you the other day?" or "You're lucky I'm not the get-even type. Not at the moment, anyway." Before you say anything, though, be sure this person did gossip. Don't assume. And don't get sucked into petty rivalries over small gossip infractions. They're unattractive, especially if you have some stature or potential, because people expect more of you. Brush it off. Try humor: "The other day I heard that I'm leaving. Wondered why I hadn't heard sooner." It's wise to remember that work isn't about sharing your every thought with everybody. Opinions change; today's friend could be tomorrow's competitor for a key position.

SITUATION 10
Belittling

A colleague of yours is predictable, in that he takes advantage of any opportunity to put you down at meetings or in small gatherings. He derives considerable pleasure from making you feel uncomfortable and, you believe, derives some power from it as well. Others appear to look to you for a comeback that will put him in his place, but you prefer to bring the conversation back to the business at hand. You're

afraid that if you gave him what he deserves, you might go too
far, and that, in your opinion, is worse than saying nothing.

Many of us would let this abuse continue until we lose control and
verbally flatten the offender. Those who are quick to anger would
be inclined to snap back with nastier insults than the ones received.
But first things first. Even in such annoying situations, take time to
assess the jokester's intentions. Is the insult or offense purposeful or
inadvertent? Does he do this to other people as well? Have you spoken with him about it and insisted that he leave personal or offensive comments about you out of public venues? In other words,
have you done some work to accurately assess what is causing his
behavior? Perhaps you'll discover that he thinks his humor is a way
of bonding, although that seems unlikely in this scenario. Perhaps
he's nervous, jealous, or truly politically inept.

If he's inept, you need to educate him, unless you want to "give
him enough rope to hang himself" by waiting to see if he insults the
wrong person—someone in position to end his pranks. Otherwise,
you might let him know that there are two levels of talk going on at
meetings: one that focuses on the task, another that focuses on relationships. Explain that he appears to be crossing over to the relationship side too frequently and at inappropriate times. Tell him
that, at best, his quips are inappropriate and, at worst, insulting.
Then ask him what he intends to do about it. See if he comes up
with a solution. Taking this approach allows you to avoid giving him
an ultimatum.

If he is belittling you on purpose to gain some advantage for
himself, then education isn't the appropriate route. You need to
meet with him before the next meeting. Review with him your observations and then tell him you see two choices: Either he stops
this behavior immediately, or you'll be forced to do something
about it. This is a threat, but it's a private one. You haven't made a
scene or done anything to put him in jeopardy so your actions are
still within the parameters of positive politics. In fact, he's lucky that
you're taking this route, and you might want to point that out. Ex-

press a desire to "get back to the way we used to work together" or "work together with respect." If respect is part of the company's value system, gently remind him of that. He should take this to mean that you are willing to move this issue to a higher level if necessary. Leave it at that and see how the next meeting goes. If he does repeat his behavior, it's time to be more direct.

A FEW TIPS FOR LEANING TOWARD POSITIVE POLITICS

These hypothetical situations are useful as practice. Without a repertoire of responses readily available or at least some sense of how to respond to challenging political situations, most of us are inclined to handle them badly. Yet a certain readiness factor for positive politics must be present. By now, after thinking about the preceding hypothetical situations, you probably have a sense of whether you're inclined toward positive politics. Maybe you'd like to be but don't know quite where to start. Some guidelines follow. If you use them, eventually you'll become more skilled at solving political dilemmas in ways that won't require picking up the bodies afterward.

POSITIVE POLITICS GUIDELINES

- Have you checked your assumptions about what the other person intended?
- When you're trying to determine someone's intent, do you use a telling or an asking approach?
- What exactly do you want to change?
- What exactly do you want from the other person?
- What can you give in return?
- How will you avoid placing blame when you want to move toward a constructive outcome?
- What events or issues of a delicate nature might you have to discuss, and how will you do so in a constructive way?
- How will you initially frame what you have to say (as an idea, a disagreement, a suggestion, etc.)?

- Are you ready for what he or she might say that could derail you?
- Is there someone you both respect who might be of assistance in working through the issue?
- How will you constructively elicit such help?
- What steps will you take to keep any and all discussions on target? Might some diversions be constructive?
- Can you make this a win-win situation?
- What follow-up steps will both of you take?
- What stopgap measures will you develop to ensure that this kind of situation doesn't arise again?

The benefit in using positive politics guidelines of this type is that your outcomes are likely to be more gratifying than if achieved by negative techniques. Damage will be minimal and relationships will be spared. People who make it to the top usually are the ones who learned how to get things done without drawing blood. As one successful media executive told me, "It takes a lot of energy for me not to engage my mouth, but I've gotten better over the years. You have to ask yourself: Do I want to get even? Is that the purpose? Do I really need to pound this person into the ground?" She shared with me a story that makes the point. "A person I'd never met was irate at hearing that I was getting promoted to a position she wanted. She began to sabotage me. She told anyone who'd listen, including potential employers, that I didn't know what I was doing. I'd never talked to her. This came out of the blue. I could have taken her on and won, but there would have been extensive damage and a lot of taking sides. Instead I arranged to meet her for breakfast, told her I'd always respected her as a journalist but that the position we both wanted called for the kind of technical expertise I'd been developing. Believe it or not, we left on good terms; in fact, we're friends now. I could have taken a different route. I'd certainly done that often enough, but that time, tough as it was, I played it smart."

DEVELOPING AN ORGANIZATIONAL POLITICAL COMPASS

If the purpose of your organization is the dissemination of values, political or otherwise, success requires conversations among those whose thoughts and actions are to be influenced. It isn't enough to clearly tell people what you want them to do long term; they need to have some buy-in, some involvement in developing the map. Making demands or using coercion may silence one side, often the larger one, perhaps resulting in short-term compliance but not long-term private acceptance. Guidelines must have meaning for the people who use them and resonance in terms of being reflective of and relevant to their experiences. Most organizations give only cursory attention to developing meaningful, resonant guidelines. For this reason most efforts at developing values guidelines are like one hand clapping; eventually they amount to another time-consuming activity of little if any utility.

If more companies were to approach the development of value systems as a process that requires ongoing discussion, organizational values implementation would be more successful. The document produced would be a living one. Before beginning the process of developing political guidelines, organization leaders should ask themselves and the people who work for them these questions:

> *What biases do we bring to the subject of politics or any value system?*
>
> *What matters to us and therefore may shape what we decide is right or wrong?*
>
> *Who should be involved in this discussion so that the product that emerges is not foreign to those whose behaviors will be guided by it?*
>
> *How can we ensure that the product is a living one responsive to the needs of the organization and its people rather than one imposed on both with no room for revision?*

Many organizations and individuals are political utilitarians. They measure their actions according to whether they'll achieve an important goal, get caught, look bad, or somehow harm the career aspirations of senior managers. In short, they focus on what works for them at the time. In his book *Church and State*, philosopher Desmond Clarke describes utilitarian thinking with regard to torturing prisoners to get information from them. The utilitarian, he explains, looks at the human suffering and degradation and possible unwelcome media attention and weighs those against gaining useful information. No higher-order thinking is involved, only a comparison of outcomes. Clarke explains: "The utilitarian then simply calculates—in a rather rough and ready fashion—whether the welcome effects of torturing someone outweigh (or are likely to outweigh) the unwelcome effects. And if they do, then the act of torturing the criminal suspect is a *morally good act*."[6]

The temptation in organizations is to be purely utilitarian—answering to no outside entity, focused exclusively on inside goals. Yet we've seen how badly that approach has turned out for businesses. Any set of organizational political values will be affected by the values its constituents bring from the outside. They can be fought or they can be integrated; the latter tends to be more effective.

According to Jim Collins, author of the best-seller *Good to Great: Why Some Companies Make the Leap and Others Don't*, companies that succeed year after year have in common a set of core values supported from the top. These companies are not utilitarian. They develop a set of values and make sure those values have support from the most senior to the most junior person. Sometimes political values derive quite readily from general values programs already in place.[7] Let's look at two successful companies that have grappled with the issue of values guidelines and how they relate to having an organizational compass.

MARS

By the 1970s, the main focus of the Mars family business fell into four distinct areas: snackfood/food, pet care, drinks, and electronics. Since then the business aim has been to build on these strengths on a global scale. As a result, Mars has grown from $300 million turnover at the start of the 1970s into the $14 billion business it is today. Mars operates in over one hundred countries and is one of the largest family-owned businesses in the world.

How do you manage the politics of a company in one hundred countries? As a former manager told me, Mars began by identifying five principles that guide "not only in what is said but also in what is done." These principles are quality, responsibility, mutuality, efficiency, and freedom. Although these principles don't specifically mention politics, they serve as parameters that discourage negative forms of political action. The manager, let's call him Peter, provided me with interpretations of each principle from which political benefits can be readily derived. For example, quality pertains to maintaining high standards for one's work. Responsibility is about discouraging cronyism and instead encouraging honesty and respect. Mutuality is about finding win-wins, shared benefits with customers. Efficiency discourages individual empires. Freedom focuses on stewardship—a responsible-to-the-next-generation kind of leadership. Peter considers Mars one of those rare companies where what is preached actually is practiced. "One reason it works," he explained, "is that it's a family company, but more than that, they keep in-fighting under control, even making their offspring work to achieve senior positions." With regard to politics, the five principles serve as "a framework that minimizes negative practices." No company can totally prevent negative politics, but Mars, via its guiding principles, and whether intentionally or not, has gone a long way toward discouraging them.

I asked Peter if political maneuverer bosses survive at Mars. His reply was considered, not a knee-jerk. "No, we don't tolerate them for a moment." Instead he said, "All senior executives need to consider an equation when someone is political in negative ways—

what's his or her ratio of effectiveness to disruptiveness. If someone is disruptive but highly effective, he or she could survive for a while. But eventually a healthy organism spits out the irritant." I said to Peter, "It can be a long wait sometimes." "No shit!" he replied. "You just have to wait until the person reaches the irritant tipping point—the point when he pisses off one too many people or the wrong one. Eventually the worst ones always do."

The responsibility principle is clearly one that gets directly at ethical politics. By consciously breaking down divisive work practices, a company ensures that politics won't become pathological and that the company won't be eaten alive by its own staff. Vigilance is important here as is consistency. I've coached and consulted in a number of companies that were less than committed when it came to actually applying principles hung on office walls. If a company wants politics to be positive, it must take efforts to ensure that people who go negative aren't rewarded. Companies should not accept deception of the ulterior-motive type. Also, as mentioned earlier, if values like those developed by Mars are merely handed down, rather than emanating from the people who will use them as guidelines, eventually they become meaningless lists on the wall.

Mutuality is another way to keep politics from going negative. Win-win isn't about taking advantage of people; it's about coming up with ways for a company to benefit while customers, including internal customers, benefit as well. Mutuality recognizes the benefit of long-term thinking. Most negative forms of politics are short-sighted, used by people who overestimate their ability to manipulate without being noticed. When they are discovered, resentment and revenge result, and the culture of an organization is threatened as the poison spreads. Mutuality discourages deception, manipulation, and coercion and focuses instead on finding a workable, agreed-on path.

The Mars efficiency principle doesn't address politics directly unless we consider how little kingdoms spring up, preventing cooperation between divisions, creating redundancy in types of work and harmful competition. Efficiency is hindered in these ways. Organizations that want divisions to work efficiently together must keep politics to a minimal or moderate level.

Freedom for Mars is largely the ability to remain a family business. "It's more complex than that," Peter explained, however. "There's a sense that the people in charge are custodians of the business. They act as if they've been entrusted to pass on to the next generation a better company." The kind of leadership encouraged at Mars is stewardship. When businesses focus only on making money, negative politics is more prevalent. Greed is at the heart of the lion's share of negative politics. Any company wishing to have a positive political environment needs to weigh the drive to be profitable against the downside of creeping political pathology, which eventually eats the company alive. Clearly Mars hasn't suffered profit-wise by its attempts at such balance. Its emphasis on freedom as a principle may not have been aimed at keeping negative politics to a minimum, but by promulgating the view of the leader as steward, the company has managed to do just that.

I must note that the five Mars principles are not for every company. They seem to be working for Mars in part because the company's leaders think like a family. Even in families, however, it's a good idea to be sure that everyone has input into the value scheme so that no one becomes a misfit. That's why even Mars should continually revisit its five principles, considering them to be works in progress deserving of occasional revision. If that happens, meanings will not only be understood, but respected and relevant to all people affected by them.

THE NOKIA WAY

Another company endeavoring to provide its employees with a political compass is Nokia, the telecommunications company based in Finland. Like Mars, it operates in companies around the world, making the task of maintaining values all that more challenging. Among the Nokia Way values are two that are particularly important in maintaining a positive political environment. The first one is respect, and that part most relevant to encouraging positive politics reads in this way:

> Treating one another with trust and respect is a corner-stone of the Nokia values, and essential for building an open and honest spirit at the workplace. Our culture allows us to depend on each other, and communicate openly and honestly.

The second component of the Nokia Way that provides a check on negative politics is a commitment to employee participation, which Nokia describes this way:

> Nokia encourages open discussion and debate. As an ex-ample, the annual globally conducted "Listening to You" employee survey is a powerful way of getting feedback from our employees on a range of important issues. We listen to the views of our employees and act on them when design-ing our people policies and practices.
>
> Another example is the "Ask HR" feedback channel on our human resources Intranet. There, every employee can comment or ask questions about our people practices and processes, even anonymously, and receive a prompt and openly published response.

This visiting and revisiting employee views and utilizing feed-back to design policies and practices keeps the guidelines as living documents, as I discussed earlier. Times change, as do people and the demands of their jobs. The Nokia Way is not supposed to be the Old Nokia Way, it's supposed to be current. Certainly consistency over time is needed, but if no one ever attends to the squeak of an aging door, eventually it falls off its hinges. Better to stay on top of things by using a little oil of political acumen now and then.

A commitment to professionalism and the fostering of an I-care attitude among employees are two other aspects of the Nokia Way that discourage negative politics. No doubt there are times when these commitments are difficult to maintain for the company and for individual employees. And critics have expressed doubt regarding the ability of Nokia to do so as it becomes larger and less "Finnish." The same could be said of Mars, as it moves out of the hands of a few family members to perhaps many outsiders. Yet if a company is open to communication and committed to respect, it can weather change so long as what is preached in terms of such noble goals as respect, professionalism, caring, and listening also is practiced.

HONESTY AT GUIDANT

A company that doesn't know itself politically leaves itself open to corruption and destruction by those without a political compass.

POLITICAL ADVANTAGE #15

"When creating a political compass, you don't need to set a goal to become the 'Mother Teresa of Politics'—a model of selfless devotion to humankind—but rather to be more like her than not."

For many of us, such a high standard is at least something to aim for. But if it is not approachable, that does not mean that no standards need apply. Individuals and companies that don't know themselves politically—due to a lack of a political compass—leave themselves open to corruption and destruction by those more confident of their standards.

Ginger Graham, group chairman in the office of the president at Guidant, a medical technology company based in Indianapolis, places honesty high in her leadership priorities. Soon after becoming president and CEO of Advanced Cardiovascular Systems (ACS), discontent among employees and an increase in negative politics caused Graham to decide that a major change in culture was needed to save the company. She decided, contrary to common practice by big organizations, that she would speak to her employees honestly. In her address to the entire U.S. sales force, Graham said: "I've always heard about what a wonderful company ACS is, but frankly, that's not what I see. What I see is deteriorating morale, disillusioned customers, and finger-pointing. I see a place where R&D and manufacturing are practically at war. You folks in sales blame manufacturing. R&D blames marketing. We're all so busy blaming each other, that nothing gets done. No wonder our customers are furious with us."[8]

Graham wasn't the first CEO to tell the truth, but she was among a small number to take this honesty many steps further to influence her company's culture. She encouraged senior managers to get coaches, to tell the truth to the rank and file, to mythologize truth tellers in stories and rituals, and to police themselves in public "honesty" forums. These four standards were communicated down through the organization until openness and honesty became ways of doing business. Negative experiences weren't glossed over in newsletters and other company communications. One year senior management even asked employees for help when, around Christmastime, demand for one of their new products outpaced supply overnight. The situation was explained before a company-wide meeting. Together management and the people who actually could save the situation came up with solutions. This event became part of ACS lore, reminding employees that management asked them for help. Stories of employees who drove products hundreds of miles to hospitals after the September 11 terrorist attacks because delivery planes were grounded also became part of company lore. Although other companies may have such stories, senior managers don't often think of sharing them to reinforce standards that keep negative politics at bay.

GETTING DISCUSSIONS OF POLITICAL GUIDELINES UNDER WAY

Even if your company already has a set of principles or values from which political guidelines can be inferred, everyone benefits when people talk specifically about what type of political atmosphere is desired. Recently I was speaking with a manager about his new CEO. "The poor guy is filling huge shoes," he said. "He's following a giant, and nobody really expects him to pull it off." President Lyndon Johnson had the same problem when he tried to follow in the footsteps of John F. Kennedy. Anyone who takes the reins of a company after someone popular leaves faces a long, uphill battle. So, what do you do? First, don't impose your will on people. They'll resist. Contrary to common wisdom, don't shake things up right away. Instead, let your meaning make its way to your employees slowly, once you've begun to assess how things work. Instead of trying to control people, help them tell you what they want. Doing this will lead to a solution partly of their making, and few things are more persuasive than one's own ideas.

Encourage people at all levels (or their representatives) to anonymously post their concerns on a Web site or to send e-mails from a specific general site to a particular location. Then, when you have tons of information, set up a team to identify themes that emerge: issues, concerns, desires, and frustrations, to name a few. Among them might be: people getting unfairly promoted, the criteria for promotion is unclear or available only to some, employees feel left out of the loop in terms of important information, others feel negative politics (i.e., poisoning wells, backstabbing, nepotism, spies, palace intrigue, language games, etc.) are rewarded. From these, derive a set of targets for change, ones derived from the very people who will be involved in defining the change and implementing it.

Ask about the company's political environment and learn from the feedback, then develop guidelines based on the information—and keep the people you've learned from involved in the process. See, for example, the political arena categories in my book, *The Secret Handshake*.[9] Use focus groups or more anonymous means; have people rate where their division lies on the continuum from minimally to pathologically political, and where the company lies as a whole. I helped Pfizer do this when they were developing their positive politics program, and it led to some very fruitful discussions. Relevance and resonance come into being when you involve people in this way. Everyone partially owns the exercise and the outcomes. By involving people, the company's top leaders, who are away from the action, can learn what is really going on.

Another tack for companies to take (complementary to the former tactic or separate from it)—one somewhat less extensive than the previous one but nearly as productive—is to create hypothetical political situations and have groups of employees discuss them. These situations also can be derived from employee feedback. Develop scenarios involving well poisoning, backstabbing, credit-grabbing, excessive favors, information hoarding, ulterior motive deception, to name a few. If possible, have people at various levels of the organization create these scenarios. Invite everyone to send their views on these hypothetical scenarios and politics in the organization to a specially developed internal Web site or by internal mail. Then have some focus group meetings to deal with some of the scenarios more openly. In all cases, do not name names, and do not use scenarios based on actual occurrences. It's best to use general themes as guidelines and let specific cases be dealt with within divisions or by people with particular grievances. Once the organization becomes comfortable discussing politics, problems will surface sooner rather than later and the damage will be minimized.

I'm regularly invited into organizations to deal with potential political catastrophes. Those situations aren't suited to the kind of exercise I've just described. They're too delicate. But they do need attention. It is possible to unravel a political knot with patience, by studying perceptions on both sides, through questions, by establishing trust, by the gradual recognition of mutual contributions to the situations, and by communication between the aggrieved parties about future steps. Doing this requires expert help. Once situations have reached a crisis point, the typical manager isn't prepared to handle them. But when companies are discussing politics openly, crises occur less frequently. People have outlets and a language to use to describe what they're experiencing. "This was backstabbing, pure and simple," "I know when I'm being edged out,"

"This is a case of contrived deniability," "A more positive approach would be an open politics forum," "What we need here is political straight talk" are used in organizations where politics is not a subject pushed under the rug. If politics in both its positive and its negative forms has been discussed and managed adequately, organizations can deal with political unrest or trouble spots. Otherwise, they run the risk of becoming victims of them. Does your company have discussions about politics? Are there venues for expressing concern and for heaping praise on examples of positive politics? Are phrases useful in disarming negative politics and praising positive forms heard in your organization? If not, it's time to suggest some political guidelines groundwork.

CHAPTER NINE

THE NEW REGINALD

Reginald Strongbrow arrives at his office at 8:20 A.M. On checking his messages, he sees that two are from directors of other divisions asking for his help on projects they've undertaken. Months earlier he'd met them by working his way onto their project teams. Then he impressed them by working hard. He smiles, knowing that if something goes wrong for him in his division, these men would likely help him calm the waters or even take him onto their own staff. He'd have to get back to them later, though, as Bill Simmons (VP of operations and his boss) had left a message asking Reginald to come to his office ASAP. Reginald rises from his chair, then, thinking better of his options, sits back down. He calls Bill. "Bill, I'll be over in five minutes; just need to finish one thing." He pauses. "By the way, what do you need to see me about?"

Bill replies, "Complaints from upstairs about how long our delivery is taking on the Camper project."

"I see," Reginald replies. "Are Ruth and Ed joining us?"

"No. It's just us," Bill retorts.

Reginald removes the Camper file from his drawer. Perusing it, he notes deadlines met and missed. As he walks to Bill's office, Reginald thinks of two key points he'll make and determines what issues he'll avoid and which ones he'll suggest Bill direct to someone else. His focus will be on marketing—that's it. Not like the old Reginald, who would have tried to field all questions no matter how limited his relevant expertise.

Reginald walks into Bill's office with obvious purpose in his step. "You're looking energetic," Bill observes.

"Running every morning now," Reginald replies as he removes papers from the Camper file. He asks why the other two project team members are absent. "They said you can handle any questions," Bill replies.

Reginald sorts the papers from his file onto Bill's desk. "Any questions regarding this pile, and they'd be right," he says. "If you want the best answers on these two files, you'll want to bring them in."

Bill looks at the piles, then at Reginald, who shows no sign of wavering. "Okay, let's begin by looking at your pile. I assume it's marketing, and I hear that's the reason for delay." The real reason for Ed and Ruth's absence is now clear to Reginald, but he chooses not to pose any accusations. Their political compasses might be on the blink, but with his intact he isn't about to lower himself to their level.

"I think you'll see in this file that the role of marketing in any delays is quite minimal," Reginald replies with confidence. "My estimations indicate that we're talking about a one-day delay attributable there. Let me show you." Reginald proceeds to show Bill the calendar of marketing accomplishments, complete with in-and-out dates.

Bill looks impressed. "So, what's the reason for a two-week holdup?"

Reginald places the marketing information back in his file and then lightly taps the two other files. "The answer must be in here. But to be fair to Ed and Ruth, any delays you do find are no doubt for good reason."

Bill looks at the two piles as Reginald leans forward in his chair, saying "I have to return a call to Frank Pillar. He wants my input on a project in field compensation. If you want me to join you, Ruth, and Ed later, I'd be glad to do that." Reginald knows that Bill won't delay him from responding to Pillar, senior vice president of finance. Bill fears Pillar but would be pleased to know that he needs to rely on one of his people for help. Reginald's decision to give Bill a heads-up on the meeting rather than going behind his back or leaving him in the dark gains him credit too. It doesn't hurt to let Bill know that people at Pillar's level value Reginald's opinion so long as he isn't heavy-handed about it.

"You can certainly give me your one-minute take on what's in these two files," Bill says.

"It wouldn't be from the horse's mouth, Bill. If I have to make guesses, I could inadvertently do Ed and Ruth a disservice. Better if you ask them. If you like, I don't mind returning when you do that."

Reginald walks over to Frank Pillar's office. "Thanks for coming over," Frank says, rising to greet him. "I'm up to my ears in alligators here, and I need someone with your focus and objectivity to look at this." He hands a file to Reginald. "You seem to troubleshoot very well, and I need a fresh eye to look over this plan. I want you to honestly tell me what's good and what's bad. Can you do that?"

The old Reginald would have offered to immediately take time out of his own schedule to do as Pillar asked. He would have been obsequious and too available, giving the impression that his time isn't valuable. "What kind of turnaround time are we looking at here, Frank? Of course I'll help, but there are two pressing projects on my desk, and I need to establish some priority on all of this."

"That's what I mean, Strongbrow. You're organized. You don't spin your wheels like some people around here."

Reginald smiles. "Not much free time for dominoes," he jokes.

"If you can get back to me by Friday, I'll be a happy man," Frank says. "That's six days from now, not counting the weekend."

"That's doable," Reginald replies thoughtfully. "Friday it is." He makes a mental note to get his report on Frank's desk by Thursday.

"Thanks, Reg."

On the way back to his office, Reginald sees Ed and Ruth looking at a set of photos. Ed notices Reginald and slips the photos under some papers on his desk. "What are you two up to?" Reginald asks in a joking manner.

"Looking over something for the newsletter," Ruth replies.

"Oh, yeah. I heard about the newsletter story. Focuses on our team, doesn't it?"

Ed looks at Ruth then back at Reginald. "You weren't around for the photo," he says defensively, as if expecting a battle. Ruth nods in support. Reginald knows he could demand an explanation for their decision to take a team photo without him. He could even demand an apology. But what would that serve? Reginald asks himself. He has bigger fish to fry. No need to make them look any worse than they do. "When is the deadline for the story?" he asks calmly.

"Soon," Ruth says, looking at Ed for confirmation.

"Listen," Reginald says, "I'm here today, you're both here, and so is Bill, so let's retake the photo. No need to leave any team member out—or the boss either."

Ruth and Ed merely stare at Reginald until he raises his eyebrows, inviting a response.

"Oh, yes, sure," Ed says. "I'll arrange it."

Reginald begins to move on. "Great. I'll see you later then. Need to straighten my tie." He smiles and turns to walk into his office.

At 6 P.M., as he prepares to leave for the day, Bill Simmons appears in the doorway. "Pillar thinks you walk on water."

"I'm just glad to help him out. He doesn't mind waiting until I finish our two projects, and he's a good guy who may be helpful to us someday." Reginald's reference to "us" was purposeful. No need to give Bill any reason to think he's defecting. He doesn't mention the second director's call. No reason to get Bill nervous about an underling making too many high-level contacts, especially, Reginald tells himself, as he doesn't yet know why the other director wanted to speak with him. He'd been out of the office when Reginald returned the call. When he knows more, he'll talk with Bill.

"Absolutely," Bill replies. "Give his request a high priority. Pillar isn't someone we want to ignore."

Bill turns to leave, then turns back. "By the way, John wants to go on the Japan trip next month. I know you've been planning to go, but—"

"I have been planning to go, Bill, for quite some time." This is not the first time John has tried to muscle in on a key international assignment. Saying that to Bill, however, would gain Reginald nothing and might divert the conversation away from what he really wants. He waits for Bill's reply.

"Yes, I know, but John needs the experience."

"And we need someone experienced representing *us*. This is a big one, Bill."

Bill looks stumped.

"Listen," Reginald says. "Why don't I take him along, show him the ropes, and get his feet wet? That'll please him. I know he's a rising star, but if we send him out prematurely the project will plummet, taking him with it. It won't cost much at this time of year, and like you always say: Good training is worth every penny."

"All right, Reg," Bill says, relieved that there's been no bloodletting over the topic and that he can now tell John that he would be going to Japan.

As Reginald walks to his car, he feels a sense of accomplishment about the day. Bill needs his advice. Ed and Ruth will think twice before trying anything devious with him. Frank Pillar thinks well of him. The Japan trip is still his, even if he has to share it. Bill seemed pleased. He'll train John, pleasing Bill even more, and establishing the pecking order

John so often attempts to ignore. All in all, Reginald has exerted control over his life and made some very astute political decisions and useful connections. And he'd followed his political compass, despite reasonable temptation to do otherwise. Yes, he indeed landed on his feet today—not something the old Reginald did very often. And he can honestly say that tomorrow is looking every bit as promising.

CHAPTER ONE

1. Reported in a letter by Grenville Clark to the *New York Times*, April 20, 1955; also see Stuart Chase, *The Proper Study of Mankind* (London: Lowe & Brydone, 1957), 257.

2. Frank Deford, "Match Made in Heaven," *Sports Illustrated Special Double Commemorative Edition* (2004): 40.

3. Scott Simon, "Humans Would Be Smart to Adapt the Ways of Other Primates in Dealing with Office Politics," *All Things Considered*, National Public Radio, May 17, 2001.

CHAPTER TWO

1. Shakti Gawain, *Developing Intuition* (Novato, CA: New World Library, 2000), 25.

2. Cited in Rod McQueen, "Hard Truths: To Capture a Corner Office, You Have to Play Politics and Know When to Lie," *Canadian Business and Current Affairs, National Post* (September 2000).

3. Paul Ekman, *Telling Lies* (New York: W. W. Norton, 2001).

4. Jon Carroll, "Everyday Hypocrisy—A Suer's Guide," *San Francisco Chronicle*, April 11, 1983, 17.

5. Ekman, *Telling Lies*, 109–110.

6. Carl Rogers, "Empathic: An Unappreciated Way of Being," *The Counseling Psychologist* 5 (1975) 4.

CHAPTER THREE

1. Mihaly Csikzentmihalyi and Keith Sawyer, "Creative Insight: The Social Dimension of a Solitary Moment," in R. Sternberg and Janet E. Davidson, eds., *The Nature of Insight* (Cambridge, MA: MIT Press, 1995).

2. Bernard J. Lonergan, *Insight: A Study of Human Understanding*, 2nd ed. (London: Longman's, 1968).

3. Kathleen Kelley Reardon, *The Secret Handshake* (New York: Currency Doubleday, 2000).

4. James Druckman, "On the Limits of Framing Effects: Who Can Frame?" *Journal of Politics* 63, no. 4, (November 2001): 1041–1066.

5. Erving Goffman, *The Presentation of Self in Everyday Life* (Garden City, NY: Doubleday, 1959).

CHAPTER FOUR

1. "New York's World Beating New Stadium," *Literary Digest*, April 28, 1923.

2. Chris Argyris, "Good Communication that Blocks Learning," *Harvard Business Review* (July–August 1994) 76–85.

3. George Anders, *Perfect Enough: Carly Fiorina and the Reinvention of Hewlett-Packard* (New York: Portfolio-Penguin, 2003).

4. Ben Elgin, "The Inside Story of Carly's Ouster," *Business Week*, February 21, 2005.

5. Warren Bennis, "No Lone Rangers," May 23, 2003, available at Cioinsight.com.

6. See Sallie Hofmeister, Claudia Eller, and Edmund Sanders, "Consensus-Building Skills Help Parsons Land Top Job; Profile: The New CEO of AOL Time Warner Is Described as a Peacemaking Diplomat," *Los Angeles Times*, December 7, 2001.

7. Edward Walsh and David A. Vise, "Louis Freeh to Resign as Director of the FBI," *Washington Post*, May 2, 2001.

8. Quoted in Dan Eggen and David A. Vise, "Freeh, Withstanding Crises—and Winning; Using Political Savvy, FBI Director Made the Most of Difficult Situations," *Washington Post*, May 2, 2001.

9. Ibid.

10. Edwin P. Hollander, "Conformity, Status, and Idiosyncrasy Credit," *Psychological Review* 65 (1958): 117–27.

11. Robin Tolmach Lakoff, "Nine Ways of Looking at Apologies: The Necessity for Interdisciplinary Theory and Method in Discourse Analysis," in D. Schiffrin, D. Tannen, and H. E. Hamilton, eds., *The Handbook of Discourse Analysis* (Malden, MA: Blackwell Publishers, 2001), 199–215.

12. President George W. Bush, as quoted by Richard Tomkins, UPI White House Correspondent, May 6, 2004, available at www.washington-times.com/upi-breaking/20040506-044219-4532r.htm.

13. Newt Gingrich, interview on *The O'Reilly Factor*, televised May 10, 2004.

14. Tannen, Reardon, Gilligan, others

CHAPTER FIVE

1. See Robert Cialdini, *Influence*, 4th ed. (Boston: Allyn & Bacon, 2000); Kathleen Reardon, *Persuasion in Practice* (Thousand Oaks, CA: Sage, 1991).

2. Gerry Philipson, "Speaking like a Man in Teamsterville: "Culture Patterns of Role Enactment in an Urban Neighborhood," in *Quarterly Journal of Speech* 61, 13–22.

3. H. P. Grice, "Logic and Conversation," in P. Cole and J. L. Morgan, eds., *Syntax and Semantics III: Speech Acts*, (New York: Academic Press, 1975), 41–58.

4. Kathleen Reardon, "The Memo Every Woman Keeps in her Desk," *Harvard Business Review* (March–April 1993), 16–23.

5. Cialdini, *Influence*. See also Robert Cialdini, "The Power of Persuasion," Executive Briefings Video Series, Stanford University, 2001.

6. Frank Millar and Edna Rogers, "A Relational Approach to Interpersonal Communication," in Gerald R. Miller, ed., *Explorations in Interpersonal Communication* (Beverly Hills, CA: Sage Publications, 1976), 87–103; Paul Watzlawick, Janet Bevin, and Donald Jackson, *Pragmatics of Human Communication: A Study of Interactional Patterns, Pathologies and Paradoxes* (New York: W. W. Norton, 1967).

7. Kathleen Reardon, *The Skilled Negotiator: Mastering the Language of Engagement* (San Francisco: Jossey-Bass, 2004); Kathleen Reardon, *Becoming a Skilled Negotiator* (academic version) Hoboken, NJ: Wiley, 2004).

CHAPTER SIX

1. C. Wright Mills, *White Collar* (New York: Oxford University Press, 1951), 260–65.
2. K. Krippendorf, "Undoing Power," *Critical Studies in Mass Communication, 12* no. 2 (1995): 101–32.
3. See Gilbert W. Fairholm, *Organizational Power Politics* (Westport, CT: Praeger, 1993), 41.
4. Derived from S. W. Schneider, *The Reengineering Alternative* (New York: Irwin Professional Publications, 1994).
5. Erving Goffman, *Interaction Ritual: Essays on Face to Face Behavior* (Garden City, NY: Anchor, 1967), 5.
6. Power, Brenda, article, *Sunday Tribune* (Dublin) June 17, 2001, 9.
7. Jeffrey Pfeffer, *Power in Organizations* (Boston: Pitman, 1981).
8. Albert A. Cannella Jr. and Wei Shen, "So Close and Yet So Far: Promotion versus Exit for CEO Heirs Apparent, *Academy of Management* 44, no. 2 (2001): 253.
9. Larry Greiner, Thomas Cummings, and Arvind Bhambri, "When New CEOs Succeed and Fail: 4-D Theory of Strategic Transformation," manuscript, University of Southern California, November 15, 2002, 6.
10. Harriet Rubin, "Desperately Seeking Vernon," *Fast Company* 61 (August 2002): 100.
11. Kathleen Reardon, *The Skilled Negotiator: Mastering the Language of Engagement* (San Francisco: Jossey-Bass, 2004).
12. Michel Foucault, *Power: Essential Works of Foucault 1954–1984, Vol. 3*, James D. Faubion, ed. (London: Penguin, 1994).
13. Michael R. Lissack and Kurt A. Richardson, "Models without Morals: Toward the Ethical Use of Business Models," *Emergence* 5, no. 2 (2003): 72–102.

14. Jean Lipman-Blumen, *Remarks at Festschrift for Warren Bennis*, Marina del Ray, CA, May 6, 2000.

15. J. H. Frost and W. W. Wilmot, *Interpersonal Conflict* (Dubuque: IA: Wm. C. Brown, 1978).

16. Robert J. Lahm, *The Phenomenon of Interpersonal Chemistry in the Hiring Process: Toward the Development of a Theory*, Ph.D. dissertation, Georgia State University, Atlanta, 1999, 233.

17. Ibid., 233.

18. Ibid., 227.

19. Blake E. Ashforth and Fred A. Mael, "The Power of Resistance: Sustaining Valued Authorities," in Roderick M. Kramer and Margaret A. Neale, eds., *Power and Influence in Organizations* (Thousand Oaks, CA: Sage Publications, 1998), pp. 89–119.

20. M. Olekalns and P. L. Smith, "Understanding Optimal Outcomes: The Role of Strategy Sequences in Competitive Negotiations," *Human Communication Research* 26, no. 4 (2000): 527–57.

21. Robert Greene, *Power* (New York: Penguin Books, 2000), 52.

CHAPTER SEVEN

1. Kenneth R. Timmerman, "Libya makes overtures to U.S.," *Insight on the News*, March 3, 2004.

2. Kathleen Reardon, *They Don't Get It, Do They? Communication in the Workplace—Closing the Gap Between Women and Men* (New York: Little, Brown, 1995).

3. Mihaly Csikszentmihalyi, *Good Business: Leadership, Flow, and the Making of Meaning* (London: Penguin Books, 2003).

4. Pete Hamill, "Henry B. Gonzalez," in Caroline Kennedy, ed., *Profiles in Courage for Our Time* (New York: Hyperion, 2002).

5. Ibid., 88.

6. Jean Piaget, *The Child's Conception of the World* (Totowa, N.J.: Littlefield, Adams, 1969).

7. Stephen L. Carter, *Integrity* (New York: Basic Books, 1996).

8. Ralph Keyes, *The Wit and Wisdom of Harry Truman* (New York: Gramercy Books, 1999).

9. Desmond Tutu, "Leadership," Report of the Carnegie Commission on Preventing Deadly Conflict, Carnegie Corporation of New York, 1998, http://wwics.si.edu/subsites/ccpdc/pubs/essays/essays.htm# leadershiptutu.

10. Claudia Kennedy, *Generally Speaking* (New York: Warner Books, 2001).

CHAPTER EIGHT

1. Kenneth Woodward with Susan Miller, "What Is Virtue?" *Newsweek*, June 13, 1994, pp. 38–39.

2. James Q. Wilson, *The Moral Sense* (New York: Free Press, 1993).

3. Edwin P. Hollander, "Conformity Status and Idiosyncracy Credit," *Psychological Review* 65, 1958, 117–27.

4. Jules Rotter, "Generalized Expectations for Internal versus External Control of Reinforcement," *Psychological Monographs* 80, 1966.

5. Ibid.

6. Desmond M. Clarke, *Church and State* (Cork: Cork University Press, 1984), 36.

7. Jim Collins, *Good to Great: Why Some Companies Make the Leap and Others Don't* (New York: HarperBusiness, 2001).

8. Ginger Graham, "If You Want Honesty, Break Some Rules," *Harvard Business Review* (April 2002): 42–47.

9. Kathleen Reardon, *The Secret Handshake* (New York: Currency Doubleday, 2001).